LONG SHOT

Steve Nash's Journey to the NBA

Jeff Rud

POLESTAR

BOOK PUBLISHERS

Long Shot: Steve Nash's Journey to the NBA

Polestar Book Publishers acknowledges ongoing support from the publishing programs of the Canada Council, the British Columbia Ministry of Small Business, Tourism and Culture, and the Department of Canadian Heritage.

Cover design by Jim Brennan
Cover photographs: action shot by Don Smith, courtesy of Santa Clara Sports Information; portrait by Andy Hayt, courtesy of NBA Photos.
Author photograph by Debra Brash
Editing by Kim Nash
Printed in Canada by Quebecor Jasper Printing

Polestar sports titles make perfect fundraisers for schools, teams and sport organizations. Contact us at the address below for more information.

CANADIAN CATALOGUING IN PUBLICATION DATA
Rud, Jeff, 1960-
        Long shot
ISBN 1-896095-16-X
        1. Nash, Steve, 1974- 2. Basketball players—Biography. I. Title.
GV884.N37R82 1996 796.323'092 C96-910414-6

POLESTAR BOOK PUBLISHERS
1011 Commercial Drive
Second Floor
Vancouver, BC
Canada V5L 3X1
(604) 251-9718 / Fax (604) 251-9738

10 9 8 7 6 5 4 3 2 1

To Lana, without whose love, patience, support and sacrifice Long Shot *wouldn't have had a shot at all.*

And to Maggie — Daddy can throw his 'puter out the window now.

LONG SHOT

Chapter One

A LONG SHOT

Bob Burrows had just poured himself a beer and was standing on the sun deck of his suburban Victoria, British Columbia home. It was Christmas time and Burrows was enjoying a quiet moment alone before the extended family arrived for their traditional holiday get-together. It was shaping up to be a typical wet Christmas off Canada's west coast and now, as dusk gently fell across the treetops, the rain was once again pelting steadily against the soggy grass of the backyard.

But as Burrows looked beyond his own property and into the public park that bordered it, he noticed a figure moving back and forth across the misty playground. It was a teenage boy and he was pounding a basketball up and down the pavement, seemingly oblivious to both the rain and the season. The boy was all alone, firing shot after shot at the wooden backboard and rim, dribbling the ball around his back and between his legs, practising moves that he would one day put to use in a real basketball game. Although the playground was becoming increasingly shrouded in darkness and there were no lights to illuminate the basket, this solitary figure continued to run through his workout in methodical fashion. While almost everybody else in Victoria was concentrating on the holidays, this young man seemed fixated on the beat-up metal rim that hung ten feet above the asphalt.

It was difficult to pick out details in the distance, but Bob Burrows didn't need to see the boy's face to know who this was. A longtime Victoria-area referee, Burrows was familiar with just about every high schooler who had ever seriously dribbled a basketball. It had to be Steve Nash. Burrows had been around plenty of talented and dedicated athletes in his time. He had himself been drafted by both baseball's Kansas City Royals and basketball's Seattle SuperSonics in the late 1960s. But Nash was different than any of the local kids Burrows knew. You could drive around Victoria just about any day of the year and find him, somewhere, on a playground or in a gym. He was always working on his game. Still, Christmas time? In the rain? And near darkness? As Burrows turned to head back inside, he had to smile at this kid's conviction.

"I think the difference between Steve and other kids is that other kids *think* they're dedicated," Burrows says now. "Steve is."

Dedicated is one adjective often used to describe Steve Nash's commitment to basketball. Deranged is another. The latter is the term Santa Clara University Broncos coach Dick Davey opts for when talking about the Canadian kid who rose out of obscurity to help his basketball program reach three National Collegiate Athletic Association (NCAA) Tournaments in four years. It is that derangement which separates Steve Nash from the thousands of other Canadian youngsters who have come, ball in hand, both before and after him. It is that single-mindedness which has made the difference between a Canadian kid simply dreaming about the National Basketball Association and actually living it.

The critically acclaimed book and documentary "Hoop Dreams" estimates that the odds of a U.S. high school basketball player making it to the NBA are roughly 7,600 to one. And this rather daunting estimate comes in the very country that produces 95 per cent of the NBA's players. In Canada, a country much more inclined to turn out professional hockey players, the chances of a high school basketball star advancing to the NBA would have to be described as microscopic. Until

Steve Nash was drafted in 1996, not a single Canadian high school product had played in the league in the past five years. British Columbia, a province in which an estimated 3,000 boys play on high school basketball teams each winter, hadn't turned out an NBA player since six-foot-ten Lars Hansen of Coquitlam played in the league briefly in the late '70s. Dating back to 1949, only 21 Canadian players have been drafted by the NBA, and just seven of those players have gone in the first round. Since 1989, when the NBA reduced its draft to two rounds, only three Canadians have been selected.

While the numbers quoted in "Hoop Dreams" are intimidating, the odds that Steve Nash has overcome are, by comparison, virtually incalculable. Nash's ascension to the world's premier basketball stage in the fall of 1996 brings the NBA's current Canadian contingent to a grand total of three players. But although they hold Canadian citizenship, neither Bill Wennington of the Chicago Bulls nor Rick Fox of the Boston Celtics is what you would call a true made-in-Canada product. Both Wennington and Fox played their high school hoops in the U.S. and, therefore, followed essentially the same developmental path as the average NBA player.

In stark contrast, Steve Nash's story is anything but average. Not only has he risen out of the veritable hoops hinterland of the Canadian junior high and high school systems, he has also managed to crack the NBA's exclusive 400-player club at what is arguably its most difficult skill position. A six-foot-three, 195-pound point guard, Nash has made the NBA because of his finely honed fundamentals, his leadership skills, his fierce competitiveness and his uncanny feel for the game – not because of an overactive pituitary gland.

Several factors have contributed to Steve's survival against the longest of odds. Some of his success can be attributed to genetics. He was born into an athletically superior family that begins with father John, a former semi-professional soccer player, and continues through to younger brother Martin, a talented midfielder with the Canadian Olympic soccer team. And certainly

Steve Nash's first love was soccer. His mother Jean said that, even as a toddler, he only wanted to play with sports equipment.

Steve's better-than-average size has not been detrimental to his career choice.

Steve Nash has also clearly benefited from the nurturing, positive atmosphere provided by his family. He has derived seemingly unlimited confidence and determination from his strong-willed, loving mother, Jean. He has blossomed under the encouragement and positive instruction of his gregarious father, John. And Steve has also been guided through the past five years by some outstanding coaches, good timing and more than a little luck.

But when it comes right down to it, the thing that has separated Steve Nash from the rest of the dreamers dribbling in driveways clear across Canada is plain, old-fashioned hard work. There have been absolutely no shortcuts to his game, no magical transformations. When Steve stepped up to the 1996 NBA draft podium on a steamy June night in East Rutherford, New Jersey, he was anything but an overnight sensation. Steve Nash

Brothers Steve, left, and Martin Nash pose on the soccer pitch during a childhood visit to Tampa Stadium.

probably could have been a professional baseball, hockey or soccer player if that had been the route he had chosen. He was outstanding at all three of those games and, in fact, displayed an extraordinary gift for virtually every one of the many sports in which he dabbled. But about the time he turned 13, Steve fell head over hightops in love with basketball, the game most of his close friends had adopted in the dawn of the Michael Jordan era. What began as a way to spend more time with his buddies would turn into a long-term relationship. Instead of hockey, soccer, baseball or lacrosse, Steve decided right then, in the eighth grade, that the NBA would be his career goal. Then he set about making it happen.

"I really just fell in love with it from day one," Steve says. "I always tried to have a ball in my hand and tried to maximize my time on the court."

Much has been made about the volume of time that Steve Nash has logged in the gym, from his junior high days straight through his first NBA training camp. Certainly he is the quintessential gym rat, but his success hasn't been simply a function of hours. It has also been a matter of organization. From the time he began walking, Steve has approached his sports seriously. In fact, when the family lived briefly in Regina, Jean Nash would often take her son to Eaton's to escape their small apartment in the dead of the prairie winter. Once in the department store's family room, Mom and son would play imaginary baseball, without the benefit of a ball or bat. Jean would wind up, deliver the pitch, and the rest was up to Steve. He would dig out a spot at the plate, bend his knees, take a cut at the imaginary ball with his

imaginary bat, and then proceed to run the imaginary bases. He was all of 18 months old.

"Stephen never wanted to play with anything but sporting equipment – ever," Jean Nash says. Soccer has always been the driving passion of the Nash family. This is understandable since father John hails from London and played semi-professionally in South Africa, where he and Jean moved almost immediately after marrying in England, and where Steve was born in 1974. Accordingly, soccer was also Steve's initial love – his first word at ten months old was "GOALLLL!!" – and playing the game at an early age provided him with a grounding in balance and footwork and other rudimentary athletic skills that are essential in just about any sport. Soccer also sowed the seeds for the work ethic that would eventually help him to reach the NBA.

"One day, when Stephen was about 11, he stayed out in the backyard and juggled his soccer ball for 612 touches, keeping the ball in the air off his feet, knees and head," John says, still shaking his head in disbelief. "He came into the house and he fell down, exhausted. He was always doing things like that."

That kind of determination continued and then mutated when Steve eventually turned his full attention to basketball. During his junior high and high school summers, he often played basketball for as many as eight hours a day. And when the other kids went home to eat supper, or out with their friends, Steve hit the playground alone, setting himself up with a regimented workout schedule. One day, he would assign 500 jump shots to be made before he would allow himself to leave the court. The next day, it would be 200 free throws. Steve made a schedule and he stuck with it, refusing to go home until his job was complete. It wasn't like work, really. Steve looked at it as more of a challenge. But often that challenge meant going home in the dark, alone.

When Steve felt an aspect of his game needed improvement, he would find videotape of Magic Johnson, Michael Jordan and, most often, his hero Isiah Thomas. He would study that video, playing it, rewinding and then playing it again until he could mimic Isiah's cross-over dribble or pull-up jumper to perfection. He listened intently to what television announcers said about each of his hoops heroes, like how Isiah had battled his way through Chicago's gang-ridden streets to the NBA. Steve fed off these stories, using them as inspiration for those times when he found himself alone on the court.

During one summer vacation trip to Washington, D.C. to stay with relatives of his high school buddy, Jamie Miller, the two spent their days at Georgetown University playing in pickup games. And after those games had finished, Steve still carried his basketball wherever he went. It

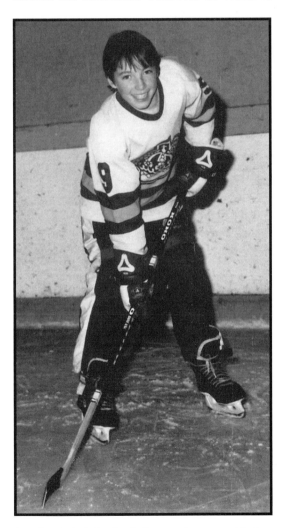

As a youngster growing up in Victoria, Steve Nash excelled at a number of sports including baseball, soccer, lacrosse, and hockey.

reached the stage where Jamie's grandmother actually began setting a place at the dinner table for the ball, nicknaming it Charlene.

Even that level of dedication doesn't necessarily set Steve Nash apart from all the other Canadian high schoolers who love and live basketball. But few, if any, continue to maintain or improve upon such a work ethic once they have achieved some early success. Even after he had become arguably the finest high school basketball player in the history of his province, Steve continued to spend more time in the gym than any other player in British Columbia. And long after he had become an unlikely standout at Santa Clara University, it still would have been difficult, if not impossible, to find another NCAA player who logged as many hours on the court. Steve's post-midnight workouts in Santa Clara's Toso Pavilion remain an integral part of the folklore surrounding his four years at the small California Bay Area school.

"Steve works harder than anybody I've ever played with, by far," says former Santa Clara teammate John Woolery. "Hands down, I mean, before practice, after practice, all the time. He makes everybody else work harder, too … And he's never afraid to ask someone else how to get better."

It was his rigid work ethic, perhaps more than anything else, that was Steve's signature as he emerged from Santa Clara as a first-round NBA draft pick in 1996. In fact, the Don Leventhal NBA Draft Report, a scouting service that rates the top 200 college prospects, included this telling passage about Steve Nash:

"You can be sure that he will not be outworked on any level."

"You know," says Santa Clara coach Dick Davey, "some people talk about goals and objectives for themselves. And with the majority of the players, it sounds good, but they don't put anything into that talk. Steve backs up his talk with the amount of time and effort he puts into becoming a player. Coming out of high school, I called him a garage basketball player."

That "garage" — or hardworking — mentality was only heightened at Santa Clara as Steve's dream of the NBA drew a little closer with each passing year. Some days, he dribbled a tennis ball across campus to improve his ball-handling. Some nights he asked Broncos' manager Antonio Veloso to unlock the gym so he and teammate Jason Sedlock could play two-on-two with Santa Clara's reserve freshmen until the wee hours of the morning. Anything to improve his game, any time.

A full year before he was drafted, Steve Nash took another major step in his development. He eagerly accepted invitations to work out with NBA players Jason Kidd, Gary Payton, Brian Shaw and Sarunas Marciulionis during the summer between his junior and senior college seasons. During approximately ten sessions around the Bay Area – including some on Payton's own backyard court – Steve was able to assess his game against some of the world's best players. It was nerve-wracking and, more often than not, Steve found himself getting schooled. But if he wasn't ready for the NBA then, Steve reasoned he would do everything he could to be ready in one year's time. Hardly surprising was the fact that after those sessions Payton graded Steve's work ethic with a solid "A-plus."

To work on his ballhandling, Steve Nash would sometimes dribble a tennis ball across the Santa Clara campus. This particular photo led off a five-page spread on Steve in Sports Illustrated *during his senior year.*

The other key to Steve Nash's remarkable journey is that he has always fiercely believed in himself. When he confided to his parents, family and friends as a 13-year-old that he planned to play in the NBA, it seemed like a far-fetched dream to just about everyone except him. But Steve refused to consider the possibility that he wouldn't realize that dream. Now his very presence in the NBA will make it easier for other Canadian kids to believe in themselves, too. To many casual observers, it was as if Steve Nash came out of nowhere to climb that draft stage on a magical June night in New Jersey. But what might have seemed like one gigantic leap was, in reality, just another in a long series of steps that had begun way back in the eighth grade.

Steve Nash at home in the bedroom where he dreamed about becoming an NBA player.

"There were so many days growing up when I said to myself: 'There's no way I'm going back to the gym right now'," Steve reflected on draft day. "Then, two minutes later, I'd say: 'Yeah, you're going to go to the gym, so that you can sit here on a day like this'. If on five per cent of those days, I had decided to just stay at home, I wouldn't be where I am today. Those extra days are tremendously important, they really put me over the edge."

Despite all those extra days, all that work, Steve Nash is well aware that if just one factor had been different, he might not have even had a draft night. If he hadn't transferred high schools and hooked up with coach Ian Hyde-Lay; if Dick Davey hadn't offered him a basketball scholarship to Santa Clara; if he hadn't had the opportunity to join Ken Shields' Canadian national team at such a young age …

"Anything's possible," Steve says of the unique path he has followed. "But at the same time, you have to be lucky. I guess the odds *were* really against me."

He is barely into his 20s, with most of his life ahead of him. What Steve Nash achieves in the NBA, and in the years beyond it, is yet to be seen. But his five-year journey from skinny, Canadian, high-school hopeful to first-round NBA draft pick, is one worth documenting. Steve Nash is indeed the ultimate Long Shot. And this is his story.

Chapter Two

A LITTLE MAGIC IN MAUI

The Maui sun had been up for only a couple of hours, but already the morning air was thick with a sweet, relaxing heat. Steve Nash leaned back slowly, stretching across a patio chair outside the oceanfront condo, and inhaled the soothing scene around him. This was an amazing place, he thought: beautiful beaches, palm trees, lavish hotels and plenty of sunshine. A little slice of paradise, and some pretty decent basketball, too.

It was mid-November and Nash's senior season with the Santa Clara University Broncos was about to begin in grand style. The Broncos were guests at the Maui Invitational pre-season tournament and they were loving it. For a bunch of college kids accustomed to cafeteria food and a steady diet of fall basketball practices, what wasn't to love? This was uncharted territory for Steve; and not simply because it was his first trip to Maui since he was a toddler. As a college basketball player, he had never faced this kind of individual attention before. Sure, he had developed an almost instant reputation as a freshman, by shooting the Broncos into the NCAA Tournament and then helping tiny Santa Clara to its monumental first-round upset of Arizona in the spring of 1993. And certainly Steve had become a marked man midway through a breakthrough junior season in which he was eventually named the West Coast Conference player of the year. Still, things were somehow different here in Maui as Steve pondered his upcoming senior season. He could feel it.

Although he had been working steadily toward his goal for more than eight years now, Steve was suddenly a feature attraction in U.S. college basketball. The change in his status had occurred almost overnight, as if ordained by some college hoops deity; as if Dick Vitale himself had descended from the mount to deliver the pronouncement: "This Canadian kid can play, Baybeeee!"

Indeed, Steve was now being lauded by the overbearing Vitale and just about everyone else in the curious world of college hoops. Tabbed by *The Sporting News* as the second best point guard in the U.S. behind Kansas star Jacque Vaughn, he was projected as a probable all-American and a first-round NBA draft pick. He was even a preseason candidate for the Wooden Award, annually given to U.S. college basketball's player of the year. Steve had spent part of the previous summer working out privately with NBA stars Jason Kidd and Gary Payton, further boosting both his confidence and his reputation. NBA scouts and management had already taken to visiting Santa Clara's pre-season practices. In fact, Chicago Bulls vice-president Jerry Krause had even sent Steve a questionnaire, including a request for some important statistical information – the height and weight of Steve's Mom, Jean. And, as might be expected, sports agents had begun circling like vultures around a fresh carcass, several of them contacting Steve's Mom and Dad to let them know that their particular agency had the Nash family's best interests at heart.

Things were happening so fast that Steve was having trouble digesting it all. But now, as he lounged outside the condo that his visiting parents and friends from Victoria were occupying in Maui's high-rent Kaanapali beach district, he had some rare quiet time to marvel at the way his life had reached its current dream stage.

"It's wild because I'm still just a regular kid from Victoria," Steve admitted to a friend as he munched on a piece of toast. "Half of me is sort of awe-struck by all this, you know, because I'm just like all the rest of the kids back in Victoria who love the NBA and dream of this sort of thing happening to them."

Steve wasn't just blowing smoke. It was really the way he felt. Just days before the Broncos had left for Maui, former Portland star and current Trail Blazers assistant general manager Jim Paxson had visited a Santa Clara practice. Jim Paxson was a guy who Steve would have been thrilled just to catch a glimpse of on the street, a player Steve had watched for several years on TV. Now he was coming all the way down from Portland to Santa Clara just to evaluate Steve. It was pretty heady stuff for a 21-year-old to contemplate. In fact, it seemed incredible that Steve was now talking, in very realistic terms, about playing in the NBA. It was no longer some far-off dream. It was less than a year away. And while one side of Steve's mind calmly reasoned that everything was happening according to his master schedule, the other side was simultaneously blown away.

"Part of me says: 'When you made this plan, you couldn't have been serious, you know?'," he admitted. "It's just sort of all worked out so uniquely and so smoothly that I've been really lucky. It makes me want to work as hard as I can every day to keep being lucky."

Steve also had to admit that there was more pressure on him at this moment than there ever had been in his basketball career, or his entire life, for that matter. The Broncos hadn't played a single game of his senior season yet and already he felt the weight of expectations from those around him.

"Who knows what's going to happen?" Steve thought. "I might not hit a shot this season."

Still, a quiet, confident voice inside reassured him that once the first game started some of the pressure would subside, like somebody opening a valve to release pent-up steam. Then he would be at ease. He loved playing basketball and his most comfortable situation in life was when he had the ball in his hands. If he was going to face some pressure, that was a pretty good place to be. On the court, it was pure basketball, something Steve had never had any problem with – no problem that couldn't be solved by practice time in the gym, anyway. But off the court, there was the unspoken pressure of exactly what this season meant to his career. A good year might lift Steve into the riches of the lottery, placing him among the top 13 picks in the NBA draft who would each sign three-year deals for as much as $3 million per season. A poor year could drop Steve out of the first round into the uncertainty of the second round, maybe even out of the draft altogether.

The Nash family had done what it could to protect Steve

A relaxed Steve Nash in Hawaii for the Maui Invitational. A terrific view, and a huge victory over defending national champion UCLA Bruins.

from the worst-case scenario, taking out a $1-million insurance policy before his senior year. The policy, with a $6,000 premium, would pay out if an injury prevented Steve from continuing his basketball career. But there was no insurance against the unrelenting pressure that every potential NBA draft pick faced.

Steve knew that many would be watching to see if he was ready for the million-dollar industry of the NBA. To keep it in perspective, he remembered that it was just a game, the game he'd been in love with since the eighth grade. But that game was quickly evolving into a business, a high-stakes business in which every mistake counted. He had been brought up to think positively and that approach had served him well. But he was also realistic enough to know that there were ramifications to this coming season. Big ones.

"It's sort of scary because it's do-or-die," Steve admitted. "Things don't go your way, it could cost you millions of dollars, when you look at it realistically."

In the soothing, sweet heat of the Maui morning, Steve thumbed through the University of California at Los Angeles (UCLA) Bruins' massive basketball media guide. It was at least twice as thick as Santa Clara's and it carried a large colour picture of the Bruins' NCAA Championship trophy on its cover. Steve flashed a playful smile.

"It's Toby Bailey's birthday tomorrow," he said, eyeing the details listed about UCLA's sophomore star. "I'd like to give Toby a little present."

Steve was referring to the Broncos' first-round tournament match-up in Maui, slated for the following evening on the full ESPN national network. It was a game nearly everybody saw as a suicide mission for Santa Clara. In the swaggering Bruins, the Broncos would be facing a team of athletic marvels who could outjump and out-talk any team in the country. And with plenty of talent returning, it appeared as if the Bruins had the game to back up that talk, too.

Steve continued flipping through the glossy UCLA program, not in awe but like a businessman overlooking a prospectus. "I think we can beat these guys," he said. "We're capable of it."

Had it not been in contravention of one the litany of NCAA regulations, Nash could have made a pile of money on that wager. Despite the fact the Villanova Wildcats were ranked third in the country, many people were picking the nationally fourth-ranked Bruins to prevail in this pre-season battle of the Pacific. And as they arrived on the tiny Hawaiian Island, the Bruins seemed to be picking themselves as well. Nobody was picking Santa Clara. Except Steve Nash.

The pre-tournament press conference was scheduled for 8 a.m. at the Maui Marriott on the Sunday morning preceding Monday's opening-round games, ostensibly so that coaches could then get on with their practices and some serious game preparation. Perhaps most importantly, however, the early-morning press conference didn't interfere with anybody's tee time.

The Maui Invitational carries few of the big-time pressures attached to, say, the Final Four or even an important regular-season conference match-up. The players spend much of their free time boogey-boarding in the warm surf, souvenir shopping or lounging in the opulent lobbies of Maui's finest hotels. For the coaches, the sweaters and sports jackets common to those chilly nights in the regular season are mostly out. Golf shirts are in. And so is golf.

For UCLA coach Jim Harrick, Maui was simply an extension of what had been a rather dream-like off-season. In the days following his Bruins' 1995 NCAA championship victory in Seattle's Kingdome, Harrick's team had, among other things, visited the White House, been honoured with a Disneyland parade and appeared on NBC's "The Tonight Show" with Jay Leno. One great playoff run that had paid off in the first UCLA national championship since 1975 and Harrick had instantly gone from a guy who some thought couldn't coach to a celebrity – college basketball's genius *du jour*.

Suddenly, the Bruins were being touted by many to repeat their NCAA championship, despite the loss of key seniors Ed O'Bannon, Tyus Edney and George Zidek to the NBA. It seemed every basketball magazine in the country carried a picture of Toby Bailey, the second-year guard with jet-powered rockets for legs who had played so well as a precocious freshman in April's dramatic national championship game win over Arkansas. By some accounts, the Bruins were going to waltz into East Rutherford for a second NCAA title in 1996 without so much as working up a sweat. Now Harrick was bringing those big bad Bruins and their current 19-game winning streak to Hawaii for their first pre-season game. And it was up to the Broncos to try to derail the UCLA Express even before it left the station.

And so, at the Invitational press conference, an informal gathering in a Maui Marriott bar that included North Carolina's legendary coach Dean Smith, it was Jim Harrick who was clearly the focus. One by one, the eight head coaches stood up and said a few words about their team and the tournament. But when Harrick's turn came, he quickly swung the focus to Steve Nash.

"He makes everybody on his team better," Harrick oozed in his easy West Virginia drawl, "and that's a great compliment to any player."

Perhaps he was simply trying to shift the focus, and the pressure, away from his team. For whatever reason, Harrick went on and on about Steve.

"I remember being at an NCAA Regional in 1993 and being out for a meal with my team somewhere," the UCLA coach continued. "We're watching the Tournament on TV and Arizona's playing Santa Clara. Arizona's got Damon Stoudamire and Khalid Reeves ... but there's this little guy called Steve Nash carving them all up out there like a side of fries. That was my first experience with Steve.

"Then I remember being an assistant coach for the U.S. at the World Student Games," Harrick added, his mouth twisting into a slight grin. "I looked up in the middle of the first half and we're down 17 to the Canadians and Nash is dishing and scoring and doing all kinds of things out there. He was just unbelievable! Those were my first two experiences with Steve Nash."

As Harrick sat down, he had no way of knowing that his third trip to Nash-ville would be much more personal, and painful. When it came time for questions from the media, the UCLA coach was asked to describe how winning his first NCAA title had changed his life.

"I've had a glorious ride, I'll tell you that," Harrick grinned. Less than 48 hours later, in the heat of the Lahaina Civic Center, that ride would end with a resounding crash.

When you step into one of Maui's few major basketball facilities, you don't think Division One hoops. The rather ordinary-looking building sits on the outskirts of the sleepy seaside tourist town of Lahaina, only 100 yards from the Pacific Ocean, and seats no more than 2,500 fans in crude bleacher-style fashion. The ceiling is ribbed with large wooden beams, evoking the sensation of being trapped inside the hull of some gigantic whaling boat.

Most of the time, this is a low-profile place that plays host to high school and youth basketball games. On many winter weekends, the most remarkable thing going on at the Civic Center is the Sunday flea market. But the spirit of the Maui Invitational quickly changes the feeling of the building. It is typically packed and rocking for all the significant games during the three-day event. When Steve Nash and the Broncos visited in the fall of 1995, all seats had been sold out well in advance. And the 800 tickets reserved for locals had been snapped up just two hours after going on sale.

Since its inception in 1984, the Maui Invitational has served up some of the best pre-season college basketball available. It also represents one of the choicest perks associated with the sport, and having Maui on the schedule can be a powerful recruiting tool for any coach. The tournament is hosted by Chaminade University, a 2,500-student private school located in Honolulu. The annual eight-team affair serves as the main source of funding for Chaminade's athletic programs.

The Broncos weren't scheduled to tip-off against UCLA until 7:30 p.m. on the tournament's opening day but Steve Nash and several of his Santa Clara teammates made their way into the Civic Center shortly before half-time of the Invitational's morning opener between the host Chaminade Silverswords and Michigan State Spartans. That game, though it would prove insignificant in terms of the tournament draw, held a great deal of interest for Steve. Prominent in the crowd was none other than Magic Johnson. A Michigan State alumnus who owns a house in Maui, Johnson was intent on catching all the Spartans action he could during this tournament. There he was, decked out in the green of his alma mater and chatting with his former coach from State, Jud Heathcote, a man for whom Magic had won an NCAA title in 1979. Suddenly, Steve Nash was no longer a college basketball star. He was a fan like everybody else. Noticing other players getting their photos taken with Magic in the teams' hospitality area at half-time, Steve couldn't resist.

"One more, Magic?" he asked hopefully before posing for a picture with one of his all-time idols.

As the second half of the tournament opener unfolded, Steve concentrated less on the action than he did stealing glances to where Magic sat with his wife and son. While Broncos teammate Lloyd Pierce sat beside Nash with headphones on, bobbing his head slowly up and down to the music and watching the game intently, it was difficult for Steve to keep his eyes off a player who had symbolized his own personal hoop dreams for so many years.

Meanwhile, the scene unfolding in the rest of the Civic Center was a vintage slice of American college culture. The most vocal fans, many of them clad in Michigan State colours and carrying green and white pompons, were an ocean and half a continent away from East Lansing, but they obviously felt right at home in this humid Hawaiian gym. "Go Green!" roared one section. "Go White!" belted back another over the squeaks and whistles and grunts of the ongoing game.

• Much of the crowd was comprised of boosters, a unique American sports animal which is known to faithfully follow its teams across continents and beyond. In Maui, most of the competing schools brought along at least 200 of these boosters, fanatic hoops fans who all stayed at the same hotel, took part in special dinners and cocktail parties and, of course, went to the basketball games dressed loudly and proudly in their school colours. It was a scene Steve had grown accustomed to in his three previous years at Santa Clara, even though it was one most Canadians would have difficulty relating to. Perhaps only in fervent junior hockey outposts such as Kamloops, B.C. could you find something that approaches the Canadian equivalent of the U.S. college booster.

There were a couple of distinct characteristics shared by this particular Maui crowd. For starters, they were a force behind their schools in ways that fans of Canadian university sports can scarcely imagine. It was a case of 24 players on

the floor and 2,500 pumped-up wannabes in the stands. Or, perhaps more accurately, it was 24 players on the floor and 2,500 head coaches in the stands.

The second thing about this crowd was that it had money. From the gold jewelry and Birkenstocks to the designer beachwear, these were people apparently wealthy enough to pick up and follow their team anywhere. And they were people who lived and died with their school's success, yearning for a chance to get close to these young athletes. Santa Clara's own booster contingent included 198 registered fans who had made the trip to Maui for Sun, Sand and Killer Hoops (the tournament's official motto).

Later that night, when Santa Clara tipped off its season, the Bronco boosters would unveil their own "unique" wardrobe, many of them sporting extraordinary burgundy and white Hawaiian shirts with gigantic pineapples emblazoned on the back. It was a definite departure from the traditional Tar Heel blue worn by North Carolina fans, and it added to the booster mosaic that would dominate the bleachers for three days in Maui.

"Sometimes you just want to play basketball and have fun and a lot of these people seem like they're counting on you," Steve said, referring to the boosters. "It is neat but it's kind of strange, too. I don't think it does any harm. Some people get older and they have a lot of money and this is something they enjoy. It keeps them busy. And it seems like it would be a pretty fun lifestyle to follow a team around to places like this."

Ironically, many of the same college athletes whom these wealthy boosters seemed to idolize were forced to penny-pinch just to get by. For this entire nine-day trip to Maui and Portland, Santa Clara players were receiving just $140 US each in *per diem*. But as the Maui morning wore on, thoughts of money and boosters were pushed into the background. The Broncos had an evening date with the mighty UCLA Bruins and that was all the incentive they needed.

By the time Santa Clara's season-opening tip-off rolled around, Magic Johnson was gone, a little disappointing to Steve but certainly nothing to dwell on. There were still plenty of important people watching, not to mention the ESPN cameras poised and ready to send this game live to millions of viewers across North America.

On one baseline of the Civic Center was a row of seats reserved for NBA scouts and management. There were 18 NBA reps at this tournament, ready to chart the progress of players such as Villanova's superb shooting guard Kerry Kittles, UCLA standouts Toby Bailey and Charles O'Bannon as well as Steve Nash. In one small group sat Los Angeles Lakers' Jerry West, Philadelphia 76ers' Gene Shue and Larry Riley of the Vancouver Grizzlies. In a way, this collection of men served as jury for these high-profile college players, a jury that actually had the power to determine their future. It was a scene that Steve would see repeated time and again as his senior season unfolded.

"You know they're all watching you," he conceded just before the tournament tipped off. "You probably make a bigger deal out of it in your own mind than it is. But for me it is different to have those sort of people around, especially when I never even got a single college coach coming around when I was in high school … It's a lot different."

By tip-off time, the Civic Center had been transformed into a salty sweatbox as nearly 3,000 fans packed the gym. In November, with temperatures outside the Civic Center hovering near the 30°C mark, the atmosphere inside was even hotter. The antiquated building's version of air conditioning consisted of one solitary, gigantic fan blowing its heart out at the top of one end of the gym. With the glaring lights of ESPN added into the mix, it was like playing basketball inside an enormous wooden pressure-cooker. Perhaps to beat the heat, but more likely in an unsuccessful attempt to attract the ESPN cameras, one particularly outgoing group of Bronco girlfriends donned bikini tops, hula skirts and body paint.

Down on the floor, the heat and humidity were unavoidable. Even though the players were only completing warm-ups, beads of sweat ran down their foreheads and off the tips of their noses as they waited in line to shoot lay-ups. Uniforms were completely drenched and ballboys sat poised with towels, ready to keep the floor safe from dangerous wet spots. For the swaggering Bruins, it must have seemed twice as hot inside the Civic Center. National champions, national expectations – UCLA was larger than life, a team that coach Jim Harrick would later say was unfortunately starting to believe its own press clippings.

For the Broncos, and their leader Steve Nash, this was precisely the kind of opportunity they lived for. With just minutes to go until the tip-off of his son's senior season, John Nash looked a little frazzled as he headed from the concession area to his seat in the Civic Center.

"I'm really nervous, because this game's on TV," he confided in his easy-going English accent. "Stephen doesn't get much exposure, so this game is really important to his future. In a sense, if he scores 40 and they lose, it's better for his future than if they win and he scores nine, isn't it?"

Steve would not score 40 that night. But what happened was even better — for him and the Broncos.

Steve Nash had been the first player on the court as the massive Bruins booster section and cheerleaders boomed out "U-C-L-A! U-C-L-A!" And by the time the teams' warm-up ended amidst the incredible swelling of heat, humidity and noise, the Broncos and the Bruins each stood huddled in their own little groups, near the half-court line. Only 15 feet separated these two pods of athletes. But in terms of size, scale and the profile of their respective basketball programs, they might as well have stood a world apart. Funny thing about college basketball, though. Upsets tend to bring even the most disparate programs closer together. Teams such as Cleveland State, East Tennessee State and, yes, even Santa Clara pull off stunners almost annually. And sometimes an opponent is just primed for a fall.

That possibility had certainly been on Steve's mind in the Broncos' locker room as he tried to break the pre-game tension. "I can't believe a bunch of yahoos like us are about to beat UCLA," he had joked just before Santa Clara took the court.

The start of the game was anything but funny for the Broncos, however. UCLA came out smoking right from the opening tip. And during the first two minutes, Charles O'Bannon and freshman centre Jelani McCoy each aggressively blocked Brendan Graves, Santa Clara's biggest inside presence. McCoy, a 17-year-old from San Diego playing in his first-ever college game, also threw down two fierce dunks and Toby Bailey added another as the Bruins jumped out to a 15-6 lead with just over six minutes gone. To the despair of Santa Clara fans, UCLA had hit seven of its first eight shots and seemed to be well on its way to running the physically outmatched Broncos right out of the gym.

"We knew they were going to make some sensational plays because they're such great athletes," Graves would later say. "But we also knew that a dunk is only worth two points. When it comes right down to it, it doesn't really matter how the ball goes in."

The Broncos embraced that philosophy as the game wore on, and they refused to wilt under UCLA's initial ferocity. Steve had missed his first two shots – a driving jumper in the key as well as a long three-point attempt with about four minutes gone. But with the Broncos sinking fast, he stepped up and nailed a crucial 20-footer off an inbounds play just a minute later. Steve followed that up with a steal a few minutes later and then promptly drained another three, this time from 22 feet out, to pull the Broncos to within one point with 12:30 remaining in the first half. Santa Clara had survived the UCLA onslaught. The Broncos were back in the game and John and Jean Nash swayed along with the rest of the maroon-clad Santa Clara crowd, caught up in what was promising to develop into another magic moment for their eldest son.

Steve was far from finished, however. Stepping deftly into the passing lane, he came up with another steal, which turned into a lay-up and a three-point play for the Bronco point guard. As his free throw rippled through the mesh, Nash already had nine points and Santa Clara held a two-point lead over the defending NCAA champions. After a brief rest on the bench, Steve nailed a 15-foot pull-up jumper to put the Broncos ahead by three. But then trouble struck as Nash was whistled for his second foul while trying to break up a two-on-one UCLA fast break.

Santa Clara head coach Dick Davey quickly subbed in sophomore Lloyd Pierce, knowing he had no chance to win the game without his star available for full duty in the second half. Steve would sit for the remainder of the half, but the rest of the Broncos played extremely well in his absence, holding the Bruins to a 12-12 draw. He did his best to lead them from the bench, too, waving a towel and wildly cheering on his teammates. At one stage, Santa Clara was up five points but UCLA closed the gap to two, at 38-36, by the intermission. As the buzzer sounded, Steve rose quickly off the bench and ran toward the locker room, exhaling deeply as he glanced up at the scoreboard. Just 20 minutes to go. Could his Broncos pull off an upset that nobody back home would believe?

The Bruins jumped out to a quick second-half lead, going up 44-40 in the first three minutes. As Steve missed his first four shots of the second half, it again appeared as if UCLA would pull away

and win this one comfortably, just as everyone had predicted.

But once again, the Broncos clawed back and regained their two-point lead. The evening's decisive series then began with 11 minutes remaining, when Steve hit hulking centre Phil Von Buchwaldt on a pretty lob pass for a lay-up. That gave the Broncos a 51-47 lead. And after UCLA's Kris Johnson turned the ball over, Santa Clara got it back with a chance to take firm control.

"Hey, let's get a hoop, right here!" Steve yelled over the crowd noise as teammate Kevin Dunne fed him the inbounds pass. It was as good as done a few seconds later when Nash found Marlon Garnett with a perfect bounce pass to set up a feathery three-pointer from the corner. Next he located a streaking Von Buchwaldt with a stunning three-quarter-court fast-break bullet and the big Frenchman converted a pair of free throws after being fouled by Toby Bailey. Garnett then canned a ten-foot jumper on yet another Nash assist to cap a stunning 11-0 Santa Clara run and the Broncos found themselves up 58-47 with less than nine minutes left.

And that was it. The Bruins never got closer than nine points after that. UCLA put Santa Clara in the bonus with four minutes remaining and Steve proceeded to ice the game with six straight free throws as the desperate Bruins had no choice but to foul him. And as college basketball opponents had discovered during his first three years with the Broncos, putting Steve Nash on the foul line is like giving away points.

It hadn't been an easy night to swallow for mighty UCLA. Bronco fans taunted the stunned

Steve Nash and his Bronco teammates celebrate during the dying seconds of Santa Clara's stunning 78-69 upset over the UCLA Bruins.

and angry Bruins with chants of "OVER-RATED." And as the tourists' sugarcane train chugged and whoo-whooed loudly outside the Civic Center, the Bruins must have felt as if they'd been run right off the tracks themselves by the Little Engine That Could.

Meanwhile, Santa Clara head coach Dick Davey strolled down his bench in the dying seconds, shaking the hand of every Bronco at least twice. As the final buzzer sounded, Steve was whisked away by ESPN's Bill Raftery and John Saunders for a post-game interview. It was the highest-ranked opponent that the Broncos had beaten since knocking off number two Providence way back in 1972.

"They're the defending national champions and any time you play them it's a real gauge of where you're at," Steve told the ESPN interview crew. "I think we worked hard. We caught them on an off-night tonight. But we played hard."

A few minutes later, in the interview room, a reporter asked: "Steve, are you surprised by this win?"

"No," he shot back. "I think that you play to win and you expect to win. I am excited because the odds were probably against us. But I'm not really surprised because we worked hard for it every day and we knew we could do it."

For a shell-shocked Jim Harrick, his third experience with Steve Nash had definitely not been a charm. But he credited Santa Clara, rather than downplaying their victory over his Bruins.

"They just flat-out beat us, there was no excuse," a quiet Harrick graciously conceded in the interview room. "They're a very experienced, talented, well-coached basketball team that's been in the NCAA Tournament two of the last three years. And they've got a terrific player in Steve Nash."

Harrick was less enthused about his own players. "That's what happens when young people read their press-clippings too much," he said as the tournament continued. "They came out and had an idea about how they were going to play this year. It didn't work, so now they're going to do things my way."

Steve's senior year with the Broncos had certainly begun his way. The final line read: 19 points, seven assists and two steals for Nash; zero points and seven turnovers for his adversary, highly-rated UCLA point guard Cameron Dollar. More importantly, the scoreboard read Santa Clara 78 UCLA 69. This wasn't just a good start, it was a great one.

"I think it's one thing to work hard and know you can do it, but it's another thing to actually do it," Steve told the group of writers who would send the story of this huge upset across North America. "A lot of schools our size get there and then don't believe in themselves. I think we've got enough experience to overcome that this year."

The win was a huge thrill for all the Broncos, but it was particularly satisfying for the Santa Clara players who had actually grown up in California, in the shadow of mighty UCLA basketball. And it was likely sweetest for Marlon Garnett, who finally got to show folks back home in Los Angeles that Santa Clara could hoop it up a little, too. Garnett, a smooth junior guard who had lit up UCLA for a game-high 21 points, knew Bruins stars Charles O'Bannon and Toby Bailey quite well, having played with them during summer pickup games at UCLA. In fact, Bailey had gone to Loyola high school, just five minutes from Garnett's house. Garnett was surprised and a little disappointed at how much trash most of the Bruins, with the notable exception of O'Bannon, had talked during the game. The loudest mouth had belonged to Bailey.

"He talked a lot, the whole game," Garnett said. "They won a national championship – OK, I respect them for that. But I thought they'd be a little bit more humble about it because I know those guys … But once they got here, Toby got the first dunk and he just looked at me like: 'You can't handle this'."

While the Broncos retired to the Maui Marriott to rest up for the next afternoon's semifinal match-up against Villanova, rest was about the last thing on the minds of their boosters. More than 50 maroon-clad Santa Clara fans invaded a bar in downtown Lahaina. After closing down that place with the help of one deep-pocketed booster's credit card, some of the party moved to the Nash family condo where the videotape of the monumental win was reviewed until 1:30 a.m.

The video was back on extended play the next morning, too, as Steve dropped by the family condo for breakfast. "You can't get too excited about that win," he said as he wolfed down a croissant, "because you've just gotta go out and play again."

Indeed, the Broncos were far from finished on the court. Up next was Villanova, which likely posed an even tougher challenge than the Bruins. Santa Clara wasn't about to sneak up on the Wildcats and their star Kerry Kittles, the returning Big East player of the year.

The gym was packed and sweltering that afternoon as the Santa Clara players filed into the Civic Center, headphones on, CD players cranked in a silent march toward their dressing room. And in the stands, the Bronco girlfriends had toned down their act somewhat, switching from bikini tops to cutoffs and white t-shirts with maroon letters that spelled out B-R-O-N-C-O-S.

Steve Nash and the Broncos would have liked nothing better than to serve up another colossal upset for their fans and the folks at ESPN, but it wasn't to be on this afternoon. Steve opened the game with a jumper just over a minute in, but that was the only lead Santa Clara would enjoy as nationally third-ranked Villanova proved too big, too deep and too disciplined for the Broncos.

The Wildcats had all five starters back from a lineup that had finished the previous season ranked number nine in the U.S. and, for the most part, they played like it. Still, Santa Clara managed to scrape back from a 17-point deficit early in the second half to pull to within four points, on a Marlon Garnett three-pointer with 9:16 left. But that was as close as the Broncos would rally as they fell 77-65 to the Big East powerhouse. Nash finished with a solid 21-point, six-assist, six-rebound effort while Kittles ended up with 23 points and 13 rebounds. The two stars embraced at half-court after it was over and Kittles said he thought Nash had a good shot at making the pros.

"Keep working hard, and you'll be there," the Villanova star told Steve.

"To Steve. Be cool and good luck. From Big Magic to Little Magic" — a picture-perfect way to cap the eventful trip to Maui.

"Our main goal was to keep Nash in front of us [on defence]," said Villanova's coach Steve Lappas a few minutes after the game. "We wanted to try to eliminate Steve from making people better. I mean, the guy was still 10-of-21, but I thought our guys did a pretty good job on him."

Steve had collected his points in this game but he had also gone just one-for-nine from three-point range. And he had committed six turnovers as several promising passes inside were bobbled by Santa Clara forwards. Those missed assists were the start of what was to become an all-too-familiar trend throughout his senior season.

"If a pass is incomplete, no matter what, it's the passer's responsibility," Steve said afterward. "The ball was really slick today due to the heat and maybe I should have held back on some of those passes."

As Steve emerged from the dressing room, he was clearly disappointed. He had believed, as had his teammates, that this Villanova team had been beatable for the Broncos, too. But his spirits were lifted somewhat by a surprise visit from Larry Walker, the Colorado Rockies baseball star from Maple Ridge, B.C., who happened to be vacationing in Maui at the time. Walker told Steve he had come to the Villanova game specifically to watch him play and he also invited Steve out to dinner. Having already made plans with his family and friends, Nash declined, but the mere invitation was a thrill. Maybe a bigger thrill, however, was the fact Magic Johnson had caught Steve's eye and smiled approvingly prior to the Villanova game. He was starting to move with some pretty impressive company.

Steve, his family and a few friends slipped out of the gym and into the silky comfort of the Maui darkness, finding a nearby pasta restaurant that wasn't too crowded for a post-game meal and visit. By coincidence, Steve Lappas and his Villanova team happened to be walking into the restaurant at the same time. Nash grinned as the two made eye contact.

"I just can't shake you guys," he said playfully to the Wildcats coach.

"Hey," smiled Lappas. "So why did you choose to go to Santa Clara, anyway?"

In the ten minutes that followed, Steve explained how nobody but the Broncos had bothered to recruit him. It was a story that seemed to shock the Villanova coach, who might have been making mental notes: "Scout Canada, scout Canada."

"You've got a good chance to make the NBA," Lappas told Steve as the two headed for their separate tables. "Keep working hard at it."

The job would continue the following day as the Broncos closed out their Maui experience with a workmanlike 77-71 win over Michigan State. Steve turned in his third straight solid game, finishing with 23 points and four assists as the Broncos led virtually wire to wire with Magic again watching from the stands. In the final 32 seconds, Steve hit four straight free throws to keep the rallying Spartans at bay.

The Maui Invitational would end later that evening for Steve, as he was named to the all-tournament team following Villanova's 77-75 win over North Carolina in the steamy championship game. Later that week, through a mutual friend, Magic autographed the photo he had posed for with Steve prior to the tournament.

"To Steve, Be cool and good luck. From Big Magic to Little Magic," the autograph read.

For the UCLA Bruins, Maui had been the kind of experience they would just as soon forget. Two days after their loss to Santa Clara, the Bruins fell 75-71 to Vanderbilt in the Invitational's consolation final. The Bruins were returning to Westwood with a 1-2 record, their two losses already equalling the total defeats of their entire 31-2 championship season the winter before. There were certainly some questions to be answered back at Pauley Pavilion.

"We always stand tall and are proud of what we do," Jim Harrick told the Los Angeles *Times*. "It's just November. They remember how you finish in March."

The next day, Steve and the Broncos loaded up their suitcases and waited in the lobby of the Marriott for the shuttle to catch their flight home. Sure, it was only November, but it had been a great trip, an amazing start to what they all knew would be a season to remember.

Less than 24 hours later, the Broncos were back to reality. Gone were the warm trade winds and sweet air of Maui. In their place were the chilling cold and rainy winds of Portland, where the Broncos would face Oregon State in a non-conference game to end their pre-season journey.

The trip had given Steve a taste of the special attention other teams would pay to him this season. It had also served as a warning of what he was in for from the media. ESPN had been all over him during the three-day Maui event, going so far as to talk Steve – who doesn't particularly enjoy swimming in the ocean – into a boogey-boarding session for the cameras that the network ran during its broadcast of the UCLA game. ESPN had also talked Steve and fellow Victorian Brendan Graves into posing shirtless on the beach, with parrots perched on their shoulders.

Interview requests were now pouring in as fast as Santa Clara sports information director Jim Young could handle them. Sometimes Young didn't even get a chance to screen Steve's calls. On the team's second morning in Hawaii, Nash had been awoken by an eager columnist calling from Vancouver at 7:30 a.m. The phone would rarely stop ringing all winter.

"I'm kind of thankful it's not me in Steve's position," Graves smiled, "I've been his roommate on this trip and I've seen all the things he's gone through, all that he has to do. I wouldn't want to do that."

Even in Portland, where the cavernous new Rose Garden seemed strangely dead in comparison to Maui's tiny hot house of a gym, the focus was squarely on Steve. The *Oregonian* ran a sub-headline in its Sports pages that read: "Nash gets top billing." That would certainly be the case for virtually all of his senior season.

"I think it's great," said Broncos coach Dick Davey of the high-pressure path his senior star had embarked on. "I think Steve will have highs and lows this season. He'll have moments when things don't go perfectly for him. But he'll weather them. He's a tough-minded son of a gun, and he won't let the pressure get in the way of the development of his team or himself. He knows the pressure's there – we've sat and talked about it. We've also discussed the alternative. Would you rather have the alternative? Would you rather have no pressure and nobody be interested in you as a player? Or would you want this pressure? He says: 'I want this pressure'."

The attention wasn't just coming from the media, either. As Steve sat in the Rose Garden stands, hand on his chin, watching Portland play Alabama-Birmingham in the first game of the first college hoops twinbill ever played in Portland's new arena, a line began to form around the Santa Clara star. A young boy, perhaps ten-years-old, worked up enough courage to approach Steve first, coolly asking for his autograph and then walking calmly away. A few feet later, the boy broke into a run toward a friend and then, with a huge smile on his face, proudly showed off the autograph. Another boy, wearing the Santa Clara number 11 jersey of his hoops hero, patiently toted a basketball for Steve to sign.

The autograph session was probably the highlight of this particular Saturday afternoon for Nash, however. Later, he and the Broncos played plain ugly but won, beating the talent-challenged Beavers of Oregon State 50-45. Steve finished with 20 points, but managed only three assists as his passes once again often seemed above the skill level of his teammates.

Still, though it had ended with less than artistic success, it had been a great trip and the Broncos would return to Santa Clara with a 3-1 record and teetering on the edge of the Associated Press Top 25. If college basketball fans hadn't heard of Steve Nash before, they likely had now.

A couple of weeks later, Steve's exposure hit an all-time high when *Sports Illustrated* featured him in their December 11 issue. Writer Tim Crothers visited both Victoria and Santa Clara to interview Steve and his family. The result was a lavish five-page spread entitled "Little Magic."

Steve was clearly thrilled. As a kid, he had grown up reading borrowed or hand-me-down copies of *Sports Illustrated*. Now he was actually featured in the same magazine – there was even a picture of his bedroom back home in Victoria. It was hard to believe. There was only one drawback as far as he was concerned. The photos from his minor hockey, lacrosse and soccer days that his father John had lent the magazine were a little embarrassing. One page of the *SI* feature carried three of those pictures of a fresh-faced Steve striking various bubble-gum card poses in lacrosse, hockey and soccer garb.

"I look like a girl in those," Steve groaned as he flipped through the magazine. The subtitle of the article read: "Canadian export Steve Nash doesn't get much TV time at Santa Clara, but he might be the best point guard in the country." In the glowing story that followed, the Steve Nash recruiting legend was hyper-extended to nearly mythic proportions. Such star treatment from an American magazine with millions of weekly readers meant Steve Nash had definitely arrived.

Chapter Three

IN A CLASS BY HIMSELF

Ian Hyde-Lay glanced up from his desk just in time to see two determined women stroll past his office door and down the St. Michaels University School (SMUS) corridor. The women looked familiar to the athletic director and head basketball coach of the Victoria private high school, but Hyde-Lay couldn't quite place them.

A couple of seconds later, Steve Nash and Jamie Miller walked through his office door. Hyde-Lay needed no help recognizing this pair. Nash and Miller were grade 11 stars at nearby Mount Douglas Senior Secondary School and two of the best young high school basketball players in British Columbia.

Immediately it clicked on Hyde-Lay that these talented 16-year-olds had been preceded up the SMUS hallway by their mothers, Jean Nash and Nancy Miller. Hyde-Lay also realized that there was only one reason for these two players and their mothers to show up at his school on a weekday afternoon. They were trying to transfer into SMUS.

Far from elation, however, Hyde-Lay felt a sudden sense of anxiety as the moms doubled back to join their sons in his office. He knew he could play no role whatsoever in their attempt to switch schools. "You have to go upstairs," Hyde-Lay stammered to Jean Nash, pointing in the general direction of the headmaster's office. "Don't talk to me about this."

As the mothers made their way upstairs, Hyde-Lay chatted briefly with Steve and Jamie. "I don't know what's going on at Mount Douglas," said the SMUS coach, "but I really think you guys should go back and try to work things out there."

The matter was completely out of Hyde-Lay's hands, but he knew all too well that he would take plenty of heat for this kind of transfer should it actually go through. SMUS had only recently been allowed to compete in all public high school sports leagues on lower Vancouver Island and there were still plenty of people in the community just looking for an excuse to get rid of the private school. The critics felt SMUS had an unfair, unlimited territorial pool from which to draw its athletes. A high-profile transfer like this would certainly stir up hard feelings.

As far as John and Jean Nash were concerned, their son's impending transfer had nothing to do with basketball, or any other sport. Steve was in dire need of an academic jump-start and SMUS, a private institution with only 500 students from grades nine through 12 and a reputation for structure and discipline, seemed to be exactly what their eldest son needed.

Steve's first high school report card from Mount Douglas had arrived in the mail less than a month earlier and the news had definitely not been good. His highest grade had been a C+ and, for the first time ever, he had received a D- in chemistry.

The marks were disappointing enough, but they hadn't been the worst part. Steve Nash's November, 1990, report card had also included a staggering 33 absences. John and Jean could only shake their heads. Their boy had missed 33, 75-minute classes in his first two-and-a-half months of high school. On many of those occasions, Steve had been shooting baskets in the gym while he was supposed to be in class.

The Nashes knew their son was headed for some serious academic trouble. Steve had always been a steady student through junior high school at Arbutus Junior Secondary. Now, all of a sudden, he was slipping badly.

John and Jean had long planned that Steve would become the first member of either one of their extended families to earn a university degree straight out of high school. But suddenly they were reading jarring report card comments such as: Borderline Achievement to Date. Improvement Needed. Something definitely had to be done.

The Nashes faced a family dilemma. Until this report card, they had believed high school was going well for Steve. It certainly had started nicely as far as sports were concerned, with their son winning most valuable player honours as he led Mount Douglas to the B.C. boys' AAA high school soccer title in early November. But his performance in the classroom had been another story altogether.

John Nash had also already experienced what he felt had been a rather disturbing exchange with Steve's basketball coach at Mount Douglas. When he had mentioned his son's troubling academic performance to Dave Hutchings, the school's new head coach had reassured John that Steve "could always go to a junior college." The Nashes didn't consider junior college to be an option.

The classroom wasn't the only place that things were unravelling for Steve Nash with his grade 11 year not yet four months old. For the first time he could remember, life wasn't going particularly well in the gym, either, as he and his former Arbutus teammates clashed with coach Hutchings.

Under Arbutus coaches Mike Sheffer and Dave

Thomson, Nash and longtime friends such as Jamie Miller, Al Whitley, Mark Kennedy, Adam Miller and John Clancy had developed a reputation for playing transition hoops, pushing the ball upcourt and simply taking whatever the defence gave them. It had been quick offence combined with ball-hawking defence and it had worked well. The Arbutus team, despite having nobody taller than six-foot-one, had freewheeled its way to the B.C. junior high school championship game the previous March before finally falling to cross-town Victoria rival Spencer.

But now these Arbutus "gym rats", with their flashy game and more than a touch of cockiness, were butting heads with Dave Hutchings, an established coach who had moved over to Mount Douglas from Oak Bay during the previous summer with hopes of creating a powerhouse program at the Gordon Head public school.

As far as Steve was concerned, the wheels had begun to come off his grade 11 season about the time Hutchings called each player into his office for an individual pre-season meeting.

"What are your goals?" the coach had asked Steve.

"My goal is to play Division One basketball," Nash replied.

"Well," he remembered Hutch answering him slowly. "I think you might have to readjust your goals, Steve. That's a pretty high level and I think you should maybe make some more realistic goals."

Steve had been flabbergasted. "I have played basketball every single day since the eighth grade for hours and hours," he fumed to himself. "And now I get to the eleventh grade, which is my big year to come out and be a star and hopefully get scholarship offers, and this guy says: 'You should readjust your goals.' You're not good enough, basically, is what he's saying. This is just great!"

Hutchings, meanwhile, believed Steve Nash *was* good enough to play basketball at just about any level. But based on the youngster's academic performance to date, the coach also felt Steve had little chance of being admitted straight into university. Hutchings also believed the junior college route was an option which would eventually get Steve where he wanted to be.

Still, with Hutchings' words, most of the good feelings Steve had harboured about the coach and Mount Douglas basketball were washed away. All that was left was a sour taste in his mouth. It wasn't so much that Hutchings had implied he wasn't good enough. It was more the fact that Steve felt the coach hadn't even tried to help him towards his goal. Steve had been prepared to hear: "Well, it's going to be tough but if you really work hard, maybe …" Instead, it had been simply: "Readjust your goals."

For the 41-year-old Hutchings, Steve Nash and the rest of these Arbutus grads were a different breed than what he had been accustomed to handling during 15 successful seasons at Oak Bay. The Arbutus kids were cocky, liked to play their basketball fast and loose and didn't seem responsive to anything from the veteran coach. "Geez," Hutchings had found himself thinking after one of the team's early practices, "I don't have any control over these kids."

Hutchings, who was already swamped with a heavy workload after moving from the gym into the classroom to teach commerce, found himself facing a major chemistry problem within his new team. Along with the Arbutus kids, Hutchings had eight returning seniors at Mount Douglas. The mix between the two groups wasn't good. The grade 11 kids seemed to feel that they were much better than the grade 12s and they probably were. The grade 12s, meanwhile, thought they should be carrying the load and Hutchings felt somewhat obliged to them. Hutchings also felt uncomfortable with the style of basketball the young Arbutus products played. Despite their obvious talent, the veteran coach felt they wouldn't be as successful at the high school level without making some modifications. But so far they didn't seem too interested in doing that. "They need to get out and play and get thumped a few times," Hutchings thought to himself.

As the season drew near, tension between the coach and his younger players had grown thicker and practices quickly deteriorated into a series of pushups for punishment. There had been a couple of practices when Steve swore Hutchings must have ordered 1,000 pushups, of which the players actually only did a handful. Practice seemed to be stopped every ten seconds for more pushups. It wasn't a good environment for anybody and both Dave Hutchings and Steve Nash knew it.

By December of 1990, their son's problems at Mount Douglas had led John and Jean Nash to their decision. They would transfer Steve to nearby SMUS, the private school where many of their friends' children seemed to be thriving. A couple of days after they had first showed up in Ian Hyde-Lay's office, the Nashes and Millers began making arrangements with the school's headmaster for the boys' transfer.

That same weekend, the Mount Douglas basketball team travelled to Vancouver to watch a U.S. college exhibition game at B.C. Place between the University of Nevada-Las Vegas Runnin' Rebels and Alabama-Birmingham. With word of their impending transfer already out in the basketball community, Steve Nash and Jamie Miller weren't allowed to accompany the Mount Douglas team on the trip and had to make their own way to Vancouver.

During the same weekend, word also leaked out around Victoria. Two members of B.C.'s under-17 select team were transferring from Mount Douglas to SMUS, including a point guard many were already touting as one of the best B.C. prep prospects of all time. The Victoria *Times Colonist* broke the news with a banner story in the Sports section under the headline: "High school hoop star switching allegiances."

John and Jean Nash couldn't believe such a fuss was being made about a couple of kids transferring high schools. The attention made them feel uncomfortable but they also felt it was worthwhile if it would rectify the problems Steve was having.

There was one severe drawback to the move, however. Both Steve Nash and Jamie Miller would have to forfeit their grade 11 seasons because their transfer, after playing four exhibition games with Mount Douglas, was in direct violation of high school athletic eligibility rules. These rules were designed to prevent coaches from recruiting athletes away from other schools and to prevent athletes from switching schools for sports-related reasons. The spirit of the rules had been severely stretched across the province in recent years and certainly two players with the profile of Nash and Miller would not be allowed to circumvent them.

Sitting out a season would be a major sacrifice, since it meant the boys' high school careers would essentially be cut in half. The Nashes knew it would hurt their son's chances of landing a college basketball scholarship, too. But as far as John and Jean were concerned, Steve might not even get into college unless something drastic was done. The transfer was the best thing.

Steve Nash's move to SMUS even made a lot of sense to Dave Hutchings once he'd had time to digest it. The young man seemed to be in need of a more controlled academic atmosphere and a distinct plan for his future. Hutchings felt Steve would get that under Ian Hyde-Lay at SMUS. He would also get a coach who would simplify his game, who would replace some of the razzmatazz and needless hot-dog tendencies with solid fundamentals.

Nevertheless, in the weeks and months that followed the transfer, rumours circulated around Victoria and the rest of the province that Steve Nash had been admitted to SMUS on an athletic scholarship, that the private school had fudged his grades to get him admitted — even that he had received a car and some cash in the deal. It was just talk, but Ian Hyde-Lay felt it unfairly blackened the reputation of both himself and his school.

Truthfully, the move to SMUS would cost the Nash family plenty. They received no break whatsoever on tuition for their son, paying $3,600 for what remained of his grade 11 year and $6,800 for his senior year. In the coming years, they would also send Steve's younger brother Martin and sister Joann to SMUS.

In fact, the Nashes sold their share in a small appliance repair business to finance those private school tuitions. A year after Steve's transfer, John, a former semi-pro soccer player and certified coach, took a part-time position coaching the SMUS boys' and girls' soccer teams to help make ends meet.

As for the issue of grades, Steve and Jamie had to pass the standard SMUS entrance exams before being admitted to the school. They spent their first few weeks at the school getting up to speed on all their subjects thanks to some volunteer help by a handful of SMUS teachers. That extra help continued during the Christmas and Easter breaks until the incoming pair had caught up.

It had been a big move and Steve was devastated by the sudden realization that there would be mostly practices and just a few exhibition games for his entire grade 11 basketball season. It hurt. But he knew it was the right thing to do.

Despite all the talk and some hard feelings that had surrounded the transfer, Steve Nash and Jamie Miller remained good friends with many kids back at Mount Douglas.

That didn't mean there wasn't a heated rivalry building between these two schools because of the transfer, however. There most certainly was. Until he graduated, Steve would hear whispers in every gym he visited. There were plenty of catcalls from the bleachers and people said things. People were always saying things.

The transfer tension reached its zenith as SMUS headed into Mount Douglas gym for the teams' first regular-season meeting since the boys' move. Steve and Jamie were ineligible to play, of course, but they were still fair game for the hecklers in the crowd as they sat on the bench dressed in the preppy slacks and blazers of their new school.

"This must look like a couple of snotty little private school snobs coming back to their old public school," Steve thought to himself as he sat beside Jamie on the SMUS bench. "It's not the truth, but that's what everyone's thinking. And me and Jamie know everyone's thinking that because we'd be thinking the same thing if it was somebody else in our place."

The Mount Douglas kids were on Steve and Jamie early, chanting: "Traitors!" and similar taunts in the direction of their two former players. The more than 200 SMUS kids who had made the trip to Mount Douglas for this game were ready, however. They belted right back, in a full, teasing chorus: "We've got Nash and Miller, We've got Nash and Miller."

Ian Hyde-Lay sprinted to the front of the SMUS section and implored his students to be quiet. The stands went silent for the moment. But the controversy never quite went away.

The rest of that grade 11 season was uneventful for Steve and Jamie. They practised regularly with the Blue Devils and they snuck in a few exhibition games as well as the SMUS Invitational Tournament. But mostly they adjusted to the SMUS school system.

That adjustment didn't come without its painful moments. Ian Hyde-Lay was forced to suspend Steve from practice on more than a few occasions when he failed to keep up with his school work. At SMUS, Nash was finding out quickly, you didn't play unless you could carry the load in the classroom.

The biggest difference for Steve between SMUS and the public system was that nobody allowed him to slide. The teachers were constantly on him to do well, constantly pushing. It was a supportive atmosphere but there were definite expectations.

Leaving junior high school, Steve had been a self-described "cocky kid", who had always got by on his intelligence and superior athletic ability. But now Ian Hyde-Lay was quickly making him realize how important old-fashioned values such as discipline, character and loyalty were and how there had to be a healthy balance between the gym and the classroom.

SMUS athletes weren't allowed to hang out or leave for home after practice. Four nights each week, they went straight to study hall for two hours. And their coach was usually there supervising. Seeing others put so much effort into his future soon began to motivate Steve to do more than simply the bare minimum in the classroom.

It was difficult that winter to sit on the bench game after game, however, knowing that no matter how hard or how well he practised, he wouldn't be allowed to play. And it was most frustrating during the 1991 B.C. AAA championship tournament in the Pacific National Exhibition Agrodome, an event in which Steve had always dreamed of playing.

The B.C. boys' AAA tournament is by far the biggest high school sports event in the province. It is the one week of the year when B.C. high school ball is moved out of the small gyms and into an arena, a time when thousands of fans watch instead of the handful normally found at regular-season games. Every player in the province longs all year to make it to this tournament. Now Steve and Jamie were there, but not the way they had always pictured. They sat at the end of the bench in the Agrodome, wearing their now-familiar blazers and ties and wishing they could be out there on the court.

What pulled Steve through this time was having his best friend beside him, enduring the same things. Both he and Jamie were confident that they'd be back at the Agrodome next year. And this time, they'd be in uniform.

There was also a piece of good news as Steve's grade 11 year concluded. His grades were officially on the mend. He had drawn straight Bs on his first full report card since the transfer.

"For all the people who tarred SMUS with the recruiting brush, it's been really satisfying to see him work hard and achieve and prove that he does have academic ability," Ian Hyde-Lay told the *Times Colonist* upon Steve's turnaround.

Nobody was more satisfied than John and Jean Nash. The big move, it seemed, was paying off.

By the time grade 12 rolled around, any lingering thoughts about the transfer had been washed away in a wave of optimism about the SMUS Blue Devils.

With Steve Nash and Jamie Miller added to an already potent team which had finished eighth in the province the past March, the Blue Devils started the '91-92 high school season as a heavy favourite to win it all. Officially, they were ranked number two in B.C. behind Vancouver College, but that ranking reflected a traditional Lower Mainland bias more than anything. The Blue Devils, missing two starters, routed College in the final of its own Emerald Tournament in early January to take over the number one ranking, which they would hold for most of the season.

For Steve, it was great to be playing again, especially on this team. The Blue Devils weren't exceptionally big, but they had enough height. They were skilled, physically strong and incredibly deep. And they absolutely ate teams up with their intense defensive pressure.

Steve Nash and Milan Uzelac started at guard, giving SMUS likely the best backcourt combination in B.C. high school history. Uzelac was a fellow provincial team player who would often be overlooked this season because of Nash's presence but who could shoot, handle the ball and play defence with anybody in B.C. Uzelac had averaged 19 points and been SMUS' best player as a grade 11 student. Now, he graciously moved over to make room for the charismatic presence of Steve Nash.

Ian Hyde-Lay was happy to see his two guards blend so well together. It would have been Uzelac's team in grade 12 had Nash, with his obvious bundle of talent and toughness, not arrived on the scene.

Up front, the Blue Devils started fellow transfer Jamie Miller, a high-flying six-foot-two swingman and another B.C. teamer, along with steady Jeremy Harris and Jan Schmidt. And on the SMUS bench was a second team that could have won the Vancouver Island championship most years on its own — younger brother Martin Nash, Brendan Barry, Chris Isherwood, Mark Grist, Ryan van Roode, Brent McLay, Ryan Green and Damian Grant.

Somehow, Ian Hyde-Lay managed to find floor time and roles for all these players. And somehow, he managed to keep them together, focused and motivated, even though most nights they had the game put away in the first few minutes.

In fact, Hyde-Lay was the best motivational speaker Steve had ever heard. He could certainly rant and rave like any other coach. But after dressing down a player, he would always build him back up. He was a good communicator and he always managed to provide his ultra-talented team with a challenge.

The school and the public had responded to this SMUS juggernaut as well. Nearly every game the Blue Devils played attracted a large crowd, bigger crowds than had been seen for Lower Vancouver Island high school games in several seasons. The Blue Devils dominated most nights and they had fun doing it.

Just how much confidence this SMUS team played with was evident in Milan Uzelac's submission for the school yearbook. Asked to provide his best high school memory, Uzelac wrote: "being part of one of the best basketball teams in B.C. — ever." Uzelac had been asked for the annual submission in January, long before

SMUS basketball coach Ian Hyde-Lay provided an atmosphere in which Steve Nash and the rest of the Blue Devils thrived.

the Blue Devils had won anything.

Still, SMUS certainly wasn't without its strong rivals, particularly close to home. Victoria's Belmont Braves, ranked third in the province, had four starters back from a team that had finished third at the B.C. tournament the previous spring. And the Alberni Armada entered the season ranked fifth in the province.

Both Belmont and Alberni were bigger than SMUS, but neither could match the Blue Devils' overall skill or depth. The Devils' season would eventually go down as one of the greatest in the history of B.C. high school basketball. SMUS went an incredible 50-4 over a grueling schedule that included six games against U.S. competition. The

Blue Devils didn't lose a single game when their starting lineup was intact and they suffered only one defeat when Steve Nash was in the lineup.

As the season progressed, coaches and players alike lined up to sing SMUS' praises. After his team was destroyed by a 92-57 margin in front of 1,000 fans in the final of the Victoria City Police Tournament in December, Belmont coach Muzz Bryant said simply: "They were all over us. They're a fine, fine team. No wonder they're ranked number one."

Bryant's Braves would be one of only two B.C. teams to beat SMUS that season, coming from behind in the dying minutes for an 82-77 league victory in the SMUS gym in early February. But three Blue Devil starters, including Steve Nash who was out with a partially separated shoulder, didn't dress for that game.

Interestingly, three of the Blue Devils' four losses that season came during one week, with Nash and Miller sidelined and Jan Schmidt on the mend. After losing just once in their first 37 games, the shorthanded Devils fell to Harry Ainlay of Edmonton, Vancouver College and then Belmont. After the Belmont loss, this SMUS team would never taste defeat again.

The Alberni Armada also threw a couple of scares into the Blue Devils that season. In the final of their own Totem Classic tournament at Port Alberni, with 800 fans packed into the gym, the Armada overcame an 18-point deficit and took a one-point lead with four minutes left. But SMUS prevailed to win 78-69 and up its record to 23-1. At this point, in early January, SMUS, Alberni and Belmont were ranked 1-2-3 in the province, creating the kind of interest in high school basketball that hadn't been seen on Vancouver Island since the late '70s.

The Armada might well have posed the most serious threat to SMUS' B.C. title hopes had starting forward Steve Seredick not been lost for the season with knee ligament damage sustained during the Encore Invitational staged over the Christmas break in Tucson, Arizona.

The only other SMUS loss of the season also came during that 24-team Tucson tournament. In fact, it was the only official game Steve Nash would lose as a high school player as the Blue Devils fell by seven points to East Anchorage, Alaska in a semifinal match-up. But even in that loss, SMUS was without centre Jan Schmidt and hobbling severely after Mark Grist and Jamie Miller collided in warm-up and each required several stitches.

Mostly this season was about pure domination for the Blue Devils. A terrific indication of their strength came during the second round of their own SMUS Invitational in January. The Blue Devils managed to blast the W.J. Mouat Hawks of Abbotsford 95-51 despite missing Steve Nash, having just two starters available and only six players dressed in total. So confident were the Blue Devils that despite being severely short-handed they ran the ball the entire game.

As the Blue Devils marched steadily toward the Agrodome, Ian Hyde-Lay was busy helping Steve fine-tune his individual game. Hyde-Lay had never seen a player work as hard at improving.

Countless hours shooting in the gym made Steve Nash B.C.'s outstanding high school player in 1991-92.

He couldn't open the gym early enough for Steve most Saturday and Sunday mornings. The two would work for hours on fundamentals, especially footwork and shooting mechanics.

During these individual sweat sessions, Hyde-Lay stressed to Steve the virtue of being under control. Rather than always taking the ball to the hoop, as he could pretty much do at will in high school, the SMUS coach had Steve concentrate on rocketing to the foul line and then pulling up for the easy jumper. It was a tough sell to a kid who was capable of making crowd-pleasing circus-type drives, but Hyde-Lay persisted.

"Steve, you're going to be playing somewhere next year where every guy in the paint is going to be six-foot-nine and capable of jumping out of the gym," Hyde-Lay would tell him. "They're going to throw that garbage out of there so fast. But what they can't stop is you stopping and pulling up for the jumper."

Sometimes it took a little coaxing, but Steve learned his lessons well. By the time the playoffs rolled around, he and the Blue Devils were cruising. They steamed through the first stage — the Lower Island tournament — winning their three games by staggering 77-, 51- and 45-point margins.

In the 42nd annual Vancouver Island tournament at Nanaimo's Malaspina College, SMUS rolled into the final, pounding Cowichan by a record 131-54 margin and then demolishing Belmont, the province's fifth-ranked team, by a whopping 49 points.

With more than 1,000 fans watching the next night's Island championship game in a sweaty Malaspina gym, SMUS withstood another tough challenge from Alberni to beat the Armada 80-71 in what many were billing as a preview of the B.C. final. Despite their injury problems, the Armada still posed a tough match-up for the Blue Devils, who had no concrete answer for Alberni's aggressive six-foot-eight forward Pat Cannon.

Cannon, who would go on to enjoy a fine career at the University of Victoria, poured in 29 points and grabbed 15 rebounds in the entertaining Island final. Steve Nash controlled matters, however, scoring 28 points and adding six assists and five steals to easily wrap up Island most valuable player honours.

The Island championship returned SMUS to the number one ranking in B.C. while Alberni dropped to third with the B.C. tournament scheduled for the following week at the PNE Agrodome in Vancouver. A Vancouver Island team hadn't captured the provincial AAA title since Nanaimo turned the trick in 1978, but most people were predicting SMUS would rewrite that stat in a hurry.

"There's certainly no over-confidence on my part. It would be absolutely fatal for us to look ahead now," a cautious Ian Hyde-Lay insisted as the tournament drew nearer.

The Blue Devils opened the 47th B.C. tourney by pounding the Columneetza Cougars of Williams Lake 101-46 in one of the most unequal games in tournament history. They followed that up with an easy 85-74 decision over the defending B.C. champion Richmond Colts, as Steve contributed 26 points, seven assists and ten rebounds.

The Blue Devils continued to cruise in their semifinal, blasting the West Vancouver Highlanders 94-57 in front of 3,500 fans. "What do you do against them?" shrugged overwhelmed West Vancouver coach Bruce Holmes after it was over. "We did as well as we could. I challenge any team in the province to do much better than we did."

Milan Uzelac led the Blue Devils with 25 in the semifinal win while Steve Nash had a routinely magical 16 points, nine assists, nine rebounds and seven steals. But it was the Devils' man-to-man defence that was truly outstanding as they held the eighth-ranked Highlanders scoreless for more than ten minutes in the first half.

The next night, in front of 4,260 fans in a steamy Agrodome, the Blue Devils capped one of the finest seasons in provincial hoops history. SMUS overcame a bit of a nervous start to down the Pitt Meadows Marauders 76-48 in the most lopsided championship game in the 47-year history of the tournament.

The Blue Devils led by only three points after 20 minutes but Steve keyed an early second-half run, in which SMUS outscored the overwhelmed Marauders 20-0 over a span of 7:31, to quickly put the game out of reach. And the Blue Devils' collapsing, help defence held towering six-foot-eight centre Scott Walton to 25 points only one night after the Pitt Meadows centre had dropped in 44 against Vancouver College.

As the game ended, a few small tears rolled down the cheeks of the normally stoic Ian Hyde-Lay. The win was a relief for Hyde-Lay, who had definitely felt pressured by the huge expectations on his team, but it was also extremely satisfying.

"Its going to be a long time before this school sees a collection of athletes together like this again," Hyde-Lay said. "There's been a lot of focus on Steve Nash this year, but I think we had absolutely phenomenal seasons from a lot of other guys, too. We talk a lot about basketball being a team sport. I think these guys are a team in the truest sense in that they all have put the team ahead of themselves."

Indeed, this had been a terrific SMUS team. But Steve Nash had also distinguished himself as one of the greatest individual high school players in B.C. history. His averages for the provincial tournament were impressive — 23.5 points and 7.5 assists per game — but the more telling

Coach Ian Hyde-Lay and the rest of the St. Michaels University School Blue Devils on championship night in the PNE Agrodome: A tremendous season ends with the 1991-92 British Columbia AAA boys' basketball title.

evidence was the way he had led the Blue Devils. With Nash firmly at the controls, SMUS had crushed its B.C. tournament rivals by an average margin of nearly 33 points. The Vancouver *Sun*'s post-tournament headline read: "SMU Blue Devils in class by themselves." Most felt the same way about Nash.

For his grade 12 season, Steve had averaged 21.3 points, 11.2 assists and 9.1 rebounds — nearly a triple-double per game.

"He's the outstanding player in our end of the country," Vancouver College coach Bob Corbett told the Vancouver *Sun*. "With Stephen, every time he has the ball, he's going to make something happen."

"I think of Stephen as like a Wayne Gretzky," added Belmont's Muzz Bryant in the same article. "He's very intuitive. He reads the play so well. He always seems to be ahead of everyone else."

There were also plenty of comments about this SMUS team being the best high school squad in B.C. history. Those comments didn't mean a whole lot to Steve Nash or Jamie Miller as they helped their teammates cut down the nets at the Agrodome. These two best friends were simply overjoyed to have reached their goal. In just one year, they had gone from suspended bench-dwellers to British Columbia champions. And it felt mighty sweet.

Nobody in the Agrodome felt better on this

Longtime buddies Steve Nash and Jamie Miller. Miller would go on to play Division One basketball at Colorado in the 1995-96 season.

night than Steve Nash. He had finished his final high school game with 31 points, 11 rebounds, eight assists and four steals. And as he stood at half-court during the post-game celebrations, the shiny B.C. tournament MVP trophy was firmly clenched in his hands.

Chapter Four

TAKING CARE OF BUSINESS

It was late summer in Victoria, a time of year when the sun shines, the winds blow briskly off the Strait of Juan de Fuca and basketball takes a decided backseat to pursuits such as golf, slow pitch and backyard barbecuing. It was the time of year when much of Victoria's large civil servant population is occupying itself with summer holiday plans. But for Steve Nash, it was time to get down to business.

Even though high school classes wouldn't be back in session for a couple of weeks, Steve made his way from home to the quiet campus of St. Michaels University School. He was headed there to see his high school basketball coach, Ian Hyde-Lay. He was in serious need of a game plan.

Once he caught up with Hyde-Lay, Steve didn't waste any time. With the 1991-92 school year — his senior season — less than a month away, he didn't have much of it to waste.

"I'm really interested in playing in the States. Do you think I'm good enough?" he asked his coach, a man for whom he had quickly developed an enormous respect.

Hyde-Lay didn't hesitate. "There's no question that you're good enough, Steve."

"Will you help me to get there?"

"I'll do everything I possibly can," Hyde-Lay replied. "But you've got to realize that with these big U.S. schools, they're already looking to sign the top high school players as they finish their grade 11 seasons or even earlier. You haven't even had a grade 11 season."

It was true. Because of his transfer from Mount Douglas to St. Michaels the previous fall, Steve had been forced to sit out the vast majority of his grade 11 year. He had been able to practise with the Blue Devils and he played about ten exhibition games, but as far as most U.S. college recruiters were concerned,

Steve Nash didn't even exist as a high school prospect.

Still, Steve was a little mystified that nobody south of the border had shown any interest in him. He might not have had much of a high school hoops résumé up to this point, but the rest of his on-court credentials were solid. Only 17-years-old, Steve was coming off a summer season in which he had played several games with the Canadian under-19 junior national team. He had also spent part of the summer starring for the B.C. under-17 select team, a stint which had culminated with an appearance in the prestigious Las Vegas summer prep tournament. Steve Nash had been out there for the right people to see. If only they had been watching.

Steve's best chance so far at being "discovered" by the Bobby Knights and Mike Krzyzewskis of the U.S. college hoops world had actually come during that summer tournament. It had been a terrific experience, with the B.C. team members getting ten days in Vegas playing in a competition that featured some of the top prep talent in the U.S., including future NBA stars Jason Kidd, Glenn Robinson and Chris Webber.

And while he had enjoyed himself socially in Vegas with Jamie Miller and old Arbutus buddy Al Whitley as roommates, things hadn't worked out quite as well for Steve on the court. Few college coaches or scouts among the hordes who had been drawn to the desert for this annual tournament had paid much, if any, attention to the British Columbia team or its young point guard. In fact, the standing team joke had been that B.C.'s games signaled unofficial coffee break time for the major college crowd.

As fate would have it, one missed shot by Steve had likely done the most damage to his dreams of being discovered in Vegas. The B.C. team had needed a victory over the Washington state all-stars in order to qualify for a high-profile match-up against Jason Kidd's Oakland crew, a big-time game which promised to have the University of Nevada-Las Vegas practice gym crawling with scouts.

With the pivotal game against Washington state on the line and just six seconds remaining in regulation, Steve had the ball in his hands. He quickly dribbled coast-to-coast through much of the Washington team and found himself near the rim just as time was about to expire. It was a leaning lay-up from a tough angle, but a shot Steve would have made routinely. As he released the ball just before the buzzer, he thought: "We won!" Steve could hardly believe it when the ball clanged off the rim and dropped harmlessly to the floor. Game over, and so was the chance to go up against Jason Kidd. "It could have changed my life," Steve would say much later of that single shot. "It really could have."

During that same Vegas prep tournament, Ohio State head coach Randy Ayers had been spotted in the crowd for one of the B.C. team's pre-game warm-ups. A couple of Steve's teammates, keen to finally see a "name" coach scouting their squad, pumped their fists and shouted: "Yes!" Then, with only about a minute to go before tip-off, Ayers got up and left the gym. It had been that kind of tournament for Steve. Tantalizingly close, yet not quite there.

Sure, some 15 schools had approached Nash's provincial team coach, Rich Goulet, during the

Vegas event. But they had represented mostly junior college and small college programs, neither of which interested Steve in the least. In fact, Nash hadn't even bothered to fill out their question-naires or read their literature. Small schools simply weren't in his plans.

Yet, as far as the big boys were concerned, Steve was still trying desperately to grab their attention. Long Beach State had expressed a little interest after he scored 13 points against them coming off the bench for the Canadian junior national team in an early-summer exhibition, but that had been about it as far as major NCAA nibbles were concerned.

Now, with this crucial summer almost over and just a single high school season left to make his dream work, it was time for Steve to take some action. And he knew he needed Ian Hyde-Lay's help to do that.

It wasn't as if Hyde-Lay was an expert in the recruiting field, however. In fact, the 33-year-old private school teacher was entering only his second year as a high school head coach and had never attempted to land a player a scholarship anywhere, let alone to a major Division One school.

But Hyde-Lay, a hard-working, thoughtful type who was already on his way to becoming one of the most respected figures in B.C. high school sports, knew that he had to try his utmost to sell Steve Nash south of the border. This kid had serious potential, potential that went far beyond the B.C. high school level.

After this late-summer chat with Steve, Hyde-Lay set out on an ambitious letter-writing campaign to NCAA Division One schools. By late October, he had written on Nash's behalf to some 30 programs — a list that included all of the Pacific Ten (Pac-10) teams and a cross-section of the better basketball schools from the major conferences in the U.S.

The message Hyde-Lay conveyed in those letters was typically straightforward. He didn't fool himself into thinking that the assistant coaches opening this unsolicited mail from some obscure island off the west coast of Canada would for a minute know who either he or Steve was. But his ace in selling Nash, he felt, was the youngster's connection to Ken Shields and the Victoria-based Canadian national team program. "I believe Steve Nash is a great talent, a real diamond in the rough, who has the potential to be a terrific Division One player," Hyde-Lay wrote to programs such as Duke, Indiana and UCLA. "Please don't take my word for it, though. Phone Ken Shields, the Canadian national team coach, and get a reference from him."

From those initial letters, a few schools had responded. The most interested ones called Shields for his confirmation and then in turn called Hyde-Lay to request some video tape. Seven or eight schools wrote back. Among the interested majors were Miami, Virginia, Indiana, Long Beach State, Clemson and Utah. Meanwhile, a smaller Division One program, Santa Clara University, located in California's Bay Area, had written on its own asking for videotape of Steve.

All the interest was encouraging. After a somewhat disappointing start to the summer, things were beginning to look up for Steve Nash.

It was a December day not unlike any other day in the 15 seasons that Dick Davey had spent as an assistant men's basketball coach at Santa Clara University. Davey was walking through the upper level of Toso Pavilion, home to most of the Santa Clara athletic department offices, when he heard the giggling that would ultimately change his life.

Davey poked his head inside the door of the office where the noise was coming from. Inside he found part-time assistant Scott Gradin, the junior man on the Broncos' coaching staff, transfixed by a television screen and working a remote control with one hand.

"What's up Scotty?" Davey asked, mildly interested. "What are you laughing at?"

"You gotta look at this," Gradin chuckled. "This guy makes people fall down."

Davey focused his eyes on the TV set, where a grainy homemade highlight video was flickering across the screen. The tape had arrived in the mail from Canada and it featured a slender white guard whom the Santa Clara staff had been tipped off to by a coaching contact earlier that year. On the tape, this Canadian high schooler was dribbling and head-faking his way through one opponent after another, leaving several behind like fallen soldiers on a battlefield.

The video had been shot from near floor level and was weakly lit, so it was difficult for Davey to get a proper perspective on exactly what he

was seeing. It appeared as if this Canadian kid had some decent basketball skills, but the Santa Clara assistant couldn't tell much more than that.

Aside from the player dribbling the ball, Davey didn't think the caliber of play was very good. The video had been shot in a small, dingy gym with very few bleachers and even fewer fans. And whoever had taped this action had moved the camera around sufficiently so that it was difficult to watch for very long without getting dizzy.

Still, something about this kid on the video stood out. The tape intrigued Davey enough to ask Scott Gradin to request another one from the small Canadian high school that had sent it in. Maybe the next tape would enable the SCU coaches to get a more reliable read on what they were seeing.

While Dick Davey went on to occupy himself with more pressing matters, Scott Gradin studied this made-in-Canada tape more closely. The 25-year-old graduate assistant even watched the video several times in slow motion, and what he saw amazed him every time. This kid's footwork and his ballhandling were incredible. The basketball moved along with him as if it were a part of his body. And he never seemed to have to look down, no matter what type of move he was trying to make. Scott Gradin hadn't had a whole lot of coaching experience, but he knew his eyes weren't fooling him. "We've gotta get this kid," he thought.

About a month later, in January of 1992, a second tape from Canada arrived by mail at the Santa Clara basketball offices. Scott Gradin and Dick

Davey screened it. It was far superior to the first — better competition, shot from a higher angle and this time with decent lighting. This tape showed more flowing game action as opposed to strictly highlights and it even included a few mistakes by this point guard prospect with a penchant for trying for the dramatic play. The Santa Clara assistants both felt the second tape provided a much more reliable indicator of the player's talents than the comical Canadian highlight reel they had received the first time.

In fact, as they watched this video, both coaches felt that the prospect, in his blue-and-white high school uniform, looked an awful lot like a young Bobby Hurley. "Oh boy," Dick Davey found himself thinking out loud as he watched it. "This kid's pretty good."

And so began the belated recruitment of Steve Nash, the player nobody south of the border had really seemed to want.

Nobody, that is, until now.

As the B.C. high school season progressed into the early winter of 1992, Ian Hyde-Lay's letter-writing campaign seemed to be paying big dividends. The SMUS coach had his hands full trying to ship video out to the U.S. schools interested in Steve Nash, while at the same time coaching a team that was heavily favoured to win its first-ever B.C. AAA boys' basketball title.

Hyde-Lay himself had no experience sending tapes to colleges and precious few resources with which to do so. What he managed to get out in the mail were snippets from SMUS games. This tape was normally used only for practice purposes and then discarded, but it would have to suffice for the college coaches, too.

After his Blue Devils had played a few games, Hyde-Lay and Tony Cordle, a fellow SMUS employee who volunteered as the team's cameraman, would cobble together some of the highlights and send them on their way south to schools such as Virginia, Miami, Utah and Santa Clara.

St. Michaels wasn't exactly set up to rival Disney when it came to producing these videos, however. In fact, had it not been for Tony Cordle, there might not have been any video for the colleges at all. It was Cordle, the father of a former SMUS player, who took it upon himself to capture The Best of Steve Nash on his camcorder as the winter of '91-92 progressed.

It had been Cordle's highlight tape of an SMUS-Oak Bay Lower Vancouver Island league game — played in early December — that Santa Clara and at least ten other schools had initially received in the mail. Cordle had done his best under trying circumstances, shooting a dud of a game with his hand-held camera, poor lighting conditions and no chance to move above the fifth and highest row of the bleachers in SMUS's dreary Old Gym.

Ian Hyde-Lay had known the tape wasn't going to win any Academy Awards, but he believed it was good enough to serve its purpose. "I don't care who you are, there are a few little moments in the first half of that game that make you sit up and go: 'Oh My God'," the SMUS coach thought.

Santa Clara was likely the smallest and most obscure of the NCAA schools showing some interest in Steve Nash by the mid-way point of his senior high school season. Nevertheless,

Hyde-Lay had quickly developed a special liking for Scott Gradin, the Broncos' young assistant coach. Hyde-Lay felt that Gradin, unlike many of the assistants he had dealt with from the bigger programs, could see past the competition level in Canada to the tremendous potential Steve Nash possessed as a college player.

But even as Hyde-Lay joked with Gradin on the phone about the questionable quality of the first video tape that Santa Clara had received, the SMUS coach bristled at the suggestion that the competition on it had been laughable. Sure, that Oak Bay game had been a blowout, Hyde-Lay thought, but one of the players who Steve had made "fall down" on that video had been none other than Winston Stanley, a multi-sport high school star and likely one of the top athletes to emerge out of Victoria in the last 20 years. Stanley, in fact, would go on to represent Canada in rugby's 1995 World Cup in South Africa.

"I don't care what level they're playing at, you can just watch people and tell things like their ability to see other people moving into spaces and their ability to deliver the ball at exactly the right time," Hyde-Lay said. "Whether they're playing against the School for the Blind or UCLA, it's the same — that vision and that understanding of what is going on out there is the same."

With the help of Tony Cordle, Hyde-Lay put together a second tape for Santa Clara. This time, the competition was better — action from an exhibition against the Richmond Colts and more snippets from the final of the SMUS Invitational against Victoria rival Belmont. Both games had been played at the University of Victoria's McKinnon Gym and the lighting, camera angle

and competition levels for this video were significantly better. And just for good measure, Tony Cordle even used a tripod this time.

As the 1991-92 NCAA season began down in Santa Clara, longtime Broncos head coach Carroll Williams was already thinking hard about next year. College coaches tend to do that with the maximum eligibility of any NCAA player set at only four years.

The scramble for players is a vicious one across the U.S., with coaches from the biggest programs crisscrossing the country and sometimes even venturing to other continents. These coaches spend countless hours in dusty gyms, searching out the gangly, acne-faced teenagers who just might have the potential to pull their programs up to the next level or, in some cases, even save their jobs.

The struggle for talent is particularly difficult for schools such as Santa Clara, a private Jesuit Catholic institution which is home to only 3,700 undergraduate students and located just northwest of San Jose, about one hour by freeway from downtown San Francisco.

Neither the Broncos nor the West Coast Conference that they play in are considered a pipeline to the pros, so they certainly don't have a shot at landing any of the high-profile high schoolers who are looking to make the jump to the NBA after just a year or two of college. Santa Clara also has a relatively high academic admission standard, which eliminates many other top prospects right from the start. To make matters more difficult, Santa Clara's teams are recruited and run on considerably lower budgets than those at the major basketball schools and the Broncos rarely make a national TV appearance unless they are playing in the NCAA Tournament or in a big pre-season event such as the Maui Invitational.

Consequently, the prime athletic talent rarely, if ever, finds its way to Santa Clara. The school has long had a respected NCAA basketball program, but it is usually looked upon as competitive pan-fry in a pond teeming with big fish.

That inherent disadvantage in the recruiting process was certainly nothing new to Carroll Williams. In 22 years as head men's basketball coach at Santa Clara, Williams had become quite accustomed to welcoming prospects whom other programs had passed on or mistakenly passed over. Still, despite all the hurdles, Williams had posted six 20-plus win seasons and had also helped produce a handful of NBA-calibre players, including Kurt Rambis, Eddie Joe Chavez, Nick Vanos and Dennis Awtrey.

As the '91-92 season began, Williams was keenly aware the Broncos were in need of a point guard for the future. Sophomore John Woolery was developing into a fine defender and team leader, but Woolery didn't shoot particularly well and, besides, he wouldn't be around forever. Somebody else would have to run this team in time and Carroll Williams and his staff would need to get that somebody ready. It was simply business as usual in the ever-changing, depth-chart driven world of college hoops.

Williams had initially been keen on landing guard Jerod Haase, a blue chip prospect out of

South Lake Tahoe, Nevada. But when that plan fell through early after Haase opted for the University of California at Berkeley before he had even begun his senior year of high school, Williams had targeted five other possible guard prospects. Among the five possibilities was the unknown Canadian kid, the one who would make people fall down on that funny video which would arrive soon at Santa Clara.

Ironically, Carroll Williams had been one of the few U.S. college head coaches who had actually seen Steve play briefly during the previous summer in Las Vegas. But he hadn't remembered Nash as being a player who particularly stood out. Steve was just a name to Williams, one of many names on a recruiting role call which could change dramatically from day to day, let alone from year to year.

But Steve Nash would fast become much more than just a name on a list to Scott Gradin. The eager young Santa Clara assistant had first heard the name when Dick Davey tossed it across his desk in the fall and said: "I don't know anything about this guy. Maybe you could check him out." Several weeks later, that first video had arrived, followed by the second.

Since then, Gradin had become the true believer on the Broncos staff. The other Santa Clara coaches were beginning to think Gradin was a little deranged about this Canadian kid.

Maybe he had become deranged. But Scott Gradin didn't mind. His regular recruiting phone calls to the Nash family up in Victoria had become the highlight of his week. Before long, he was raving about the personality and basketball knowledge of this Canadian prospect to anybody

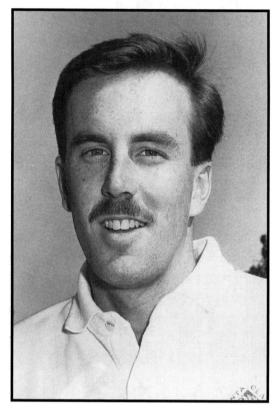

Scott Gradin was the assistant coach who was chiefly responsible for recruiting Steve to Santa Clara.

on the Santa Clara staff who would listen.

"I've got this kid who's unbelievable," Gradin told a friend who was working as an assistant at a rival school. "I'm not going to tell you who he is, though. I'll tell you he's Canadian, but that's all . . . And it's a big country up there."

While the devotion of the major NCAA suitors seemed to flicker with the winter winds, every university basketball coach in Canada would have dearly loved to land Steve Nash as the '91-92 season progressed to its conclusion. But recruiting

in Canada is typically confined to a school's geographic area. Only the Simon Fraser University Clansmen in Burnaby, B.C. have the budget or the inclination to scout extensively across the country and even the Clan is severely limited when compared to its big-time U.S. counterparts.

Simon Fraser, naturally, was after Steve Nash as his senior high school season unfolded under great expectations. In fact, before he had played even one official high school game, Steve had been tabbed by Vancouver *Province* basketball guru Howard Tsumura as potentially the greatest prep player ever to emerge from B.C. From there, the accolades had just kept rolling in.

That kind of attention naturally meant that the pressure was mounting on University of Victoria coach Guy Vetrie to keep Nash at home. Vetrie and Steve met for coffee as his senior high school season progressed, although it seemed as if the UVic coach, without the benefit of athletic scholarships or the allure of the NCAA, had all but conceded this recruiting battle to the U.S.

SFU coach Jay Triano had certainly pursued Steve the most aggressively and convincingly of the Canadian coaches. And Steve had pretty much decided that if he was forced to stay in Canada, he would end up at the Burnaby Mountain school, which at least played against U.S. competition in the smaller National Association of Intercollegiate Athletics (NAIA) circuit.

But Triano, a former national-team star who had been drafted himself out of Simon Fraser in the eighth round by the Los Angeles Lakers, was also offering this personal nugget of advice: "If your goal is to make the NBA," Triano told Steve, "then go to the States."

There was never really any question about what Steve wanted to do. There was only the question of why it seemed the vast majority of schools south of the border were hesitant even to take a look at him. Sure, Santa Clara had been hanging around for awhile, now, but wasn't that just a small school from a lightly regarded conference? So lightly regarded that Steve's SMUS teammate and best friend Jamie Miller had taken to referring to the school jokingly as "Santa Claus State."

Still, the Broncos' keen interest had served as a safety net for Steve for most of that year. He was obviously hoping for some late interest from the big schools. "At least Santa Clara's probably going to offer me a scholarship," he thought.

Meanwhile, Steve was busy burning up B.C. high school basketball with his unmatched ball handling and passing skills. His confidence surging more each day, he knew he was good enough to contribute to a major Division One program. And it was that confidence, more than anything else, which propelled him.

Steve knew that if somebody just came to watch him in person, they would want him. But inside he also realized that the bottom line was this: so far, not a single U.S. college program had shown up in person. Not even Santa Clara.

As the high school season continued, there would be plenty of personal build-ups that ended only in disappointment. Long Beach State, which had liked the way Steve had played with the junior national team the previous summer, had mysteriously quit recruiting him. Indiana, which had shown initial interest in Steve at the urging of Ken Shields, had also fallen silent. Virginia's basketball office, which had requested an additional video and had been in regular communication, called Ian Hyde-Lay to say that it was planning to send somebody to the Vancouver Island championships in Nanaimo. But when that tournament rolled around in late February, Steve's hopeful glances around the Malaspina College gym turned up no trace of a Virginia coach or scout.

Steve was more than a little disappointed by the lack of follow-up and he was painfully aware that, one by one, the major U.S. teams were already beginning to fill their scholarship quotas for the next season. He tried to concentrate on basketball and school but he had to wonder: Had sitting out his grade 11 season ruined his dream of playing for a big-time NCAA program? Or was the real handicap the fact that he was a relatively small, white Canadian and thus labeled as unathletic and unskilled, sight unseen?

By the first week of March, as the B.C. high school season was wrapping up, Santa Clara was the only Division One college still in regular contact with Ian Hyde-Lay or Steve Nash. "It's unlucky," Hyde-Lay thought. "But for a six-foot-one white kid from Canada, that's probably just the way it is."

Still, the ignorance of a few of the major programs had baffled Hyde-Lay, who wondered whether it was really so difficult for a nearby school such as the University of Washington to check out a player such as Steve. The Huskies hadn't bothered to make the effort.

One of the most blatant examples, however, had come courtesy of the University of Arizona.

SMUS had been scheduled to play in a holiday tournament down in Tucson in December and Hyde-Lay had written the Wildcats coaching staff well in advance, asking them to take a look at Steve. "You haven't shown any interest in this player, but we're going to be down in Tucson for this tournament," Hyde-Lay had written. "If it's a dead period for recruiting where you're not allowed off-campus, maybe you could send an alumnus to sit in the stands and just watch."

Steve had enjoyed a tremendous tournament in Tucson. The Wildcats, unfortunately, had not seen it. They had written Hyde-Lay back, explaining that they had filled their recruiting needs, and invited Steve Nash and the Blue Devils to watch them practise.

All the while, Santa Clara was there, like a small but faithful puppy. If it wasn't Scott Gradin calling Steve, it was Dick Davey, or fellow assistant Larry Hauser. Often, Steve couldn't keep all the Santa Clara assistants straight in his mind. They were just voices on the phone and faces in the Bronco media guide that he had been sent in the mail. "Who the hell am I talking to?" was a common thought running through his head during many of these recruiting calls.

Scott Gradin, who had been recruiting Steve the longest, seemed the most genuine. He liked to make jokes about Canada, but in a nice sort of way. Fellow assistant Larry Hauser came across as an off-beat guy, and senior assistant Dick Davey displayed an interesting geographical perspective on Canada.

"This past summer I was in Santa Barbara and this great kid from Canada was playing there. I can't remember his name, but he's from Montreal . . . Is he in your league?" Davey asked Steve, in all seriousness, one evening over the phone.

Funnily enough, that little slip had actually helped put Steve more at ease about the idea of attending Santa Clara. Prior to that, he had been somewhat concerned that he might not fit in at a school with such high standards in the classroom, a school often referred to as part of the "Ivy League of the West."

"Well, this guy's not exactly a rocket scientist, is he?" Steve chuckled to himself.

Santa Clara called the Nash home once a week, the maximum allowed under NCAA recruiting rules. Usually, Scott Gradin chatted with Steve for 15 minutes or so, before spending the next hour on the phone with John or Jean Nash. Often, Gradin would also have another Bronco assistant, or even head coach Carroll Williams, lined up to take the phone for a few minutes, too.

Before long, Santa Clara's consistent stream of calls and letters had started making an impression on Steve. He learned that the Broncos played in the same conference as Loyola Marymount and Pepperdine, two basketball schools he had actually heard of. He learned that NBA journeyman Kurt Rambis had attended Santa Clara, and that Santa Clara would be playing its second game of the coming season in UCLA's Pauley Pavilion, one of the meccas of the college game. Steve was beginning to think that maybe Santa Clara wasn't such a small-time school after all.

At one point during the winter of '92, Steve mentioned to Dick Davey over the phone that Indiana was expressing some interest in him.

Prior to Steve Nash, Kurt Rambis was Santa Clara's most high-profile NBA product. He was drafted in 1980 by the Knicks, and played for several NBA teams including the Phoenix Suns.

"Well, I'd just like you to consider that we've been here the whole time — we've been recruiting you since day one and they're just jumping into it," said the veteran Santa Clara assistant.

"Well, yeah, I will consider that," Steve thought, "but at the same time, it is Indiana."

As it turned out, Indiana never showed up.

Santa Clara, meanwhile, was always just a phone call away.

As the Broncos' 1991-92 season ended, Steve Nash had moved to the top of Santa Clara's short list of guard recruits. And Carroll Williams decided to dispatch Dick Davey, his top assistant, to evaluate this Canadian prospect in person.

It would be Davey's second trip to B.C. in as many years, after a visit to Victoria for the provincial AA high school tournament the previous spring had failed to lure towering Brendan Graves of Lambrick Park away from California's recruiting pull.

Davey made this trip after the Broncos had been eliminated from the West Coast Conference post-season tournament in Portland. He arrived at Vancouver's Agrodome, a dingy arena that reeked of horse manure and straw from agricultural exhibitions past, in plenty of time to see Nash and his SMUS Blue Devils' opening-round game of the B.C. AAA championship tournament.

As Davey watched the confident 18-year-old point guard take warm-up, he could already sense that he had found the player he'd been after for a long, long time. The way Nash dribbled the ball so efficiently and effortlessly with either hand, as if the leather was simply an extension of his body. The way passes zipped off his fingers, hitting teammates perfectly on the letters. The way this kid shot with a fluid, smooth stroke that spoke of hours and hours spent alone with a ball in the gym. And the way he led, naturally and with passion. Davey was already getting excited and the game hadn't even started.

Tip-off finally arrived and it quickly became obvious to the Santa Clara assistant that this kid was a major find. Nash and his teammates were playing against a hopelessly overmatched team from Williams Lake, and the competition level reminded Davey a little of what he had seen in that now-infamous first video that had arrived at SCU. But this initial live-game glimpse of Steve Nash was more than enough to convince the skeptic in the Bronco coach once and for all.

Sure, it was difficult to compare the high school competition level between Canada and the United States and certainly the idea of recruiting a Canadian point guard seemed a little like importing drinking water from Mexico. But as Davey sat in the musty Agrodome, he kept thinking to himself: "Hey, he can bounce it, he can shoot it, he can pass it. Those skills are definitely there. He *is* quick enough, which is surprising. He has some qualities that are unique."

Davey found himself scouring the Agrodome's mostly empty seats, wondering if anybody else from a U.S. school was sniffing around. He hoped not. As selfish as it was, he sure hoped not.

This kid could become one of the best players we've ever had at Santa Clara, Davey was already telling himself as the game continued. Who knows, Steve Nash might even be able to make a few people fall down in the West Coast Conference.

"We're highly interested in him," Davey told a Victoria *Times Colonist* reporter who wandered over to ask whether he was scouting Steve. "He handles the ball better than any U.S. high school player I've seen this year. We would love to have

Dick Davey, future head coach at Santa Clara, paid a visit to Vancouver's Agrodome to scout B.C. high school star Steve Nash.

him. We would sign him yesterday if he said yes."

The Santa Clara coach approached Steve for the first time in person after the first-round blowout was complete.

"Nice game," Davey said warmly, extending his hand to Steve. "Hey, I was watching you shoot. I noticed you seem to shoot better going to your left than to your right …"

The free advice continued over a soft drink at a Chinese food restaurant across from the Agrodome. "You know," the Santa Clara coach told Steve, "I had questions about you defensively. I really didn't think you could play defence at our level until the second half today. Then I really saw you get after it. And one possession convinced me that you can defend at our level.

"You know, if I had the papers today, I'd sign you right now."

Later, Davey approached John and Jean Nash for the first time in person about the possibility of their son coming to school in the Bay Area on a basketball scholarship.

When he returned to his hotel room, Davey telephoned Carroll Williams. "Hey, I'm going to stay up here for another day," he told his curious boss back in Santa Clara. "This kid is really good."

Davey watched one more game of the provincial tournament—a routine second-round SMUS win over the Richmond Colts — before leaving for Santa Clara, convinced he had uncovered a diamond. Now if only that diamond could remain his little secret for just a few more weeks.

Less than a month later, it was time for Steve to visit the Santa Clara campus himself. And as he left on his official 48-hour trip to the Bay Area allowed under NCAA recruiting rules, he told the *Times Colonist* that his decision about where he would go to school was "still really up for grabs."

It was a typical sunny, California spring day when Steve arrived at Santa Clara for the first time. Immediately, he was drawn to the atmosphere of the Spanish-theme campus, with its wide walkways lined with palm trees and its laid-back, California feel. Toso Pavilion, the Broncos' bubble-domed gym, was relatively small and quirky, but Steve took an immediate liking to it.

Sophomore forward Pete Eisenrich was Steve's player-host for the recruiting visit, putting him

Sitting inside Santa Clara's quirky, bubble-domed Toso Pavilion is a bit like sitting inside a gigantic marshmallow. Steve Nash was impressed with the California campus and its gym when he made his first visit there in 1992.

up for the weekend in the off-campus house in which he lived. The two hung out, played pool at the Benson Center, and joined the rest of the Broncos for a team meal. Another recruit, spindly forward Jason Sedlock from Klamath Falls, Oregon, was visiting at the same time as Steve. Sedlock seemed to ignore Steve all weekend. "A pretty arrogant guy," Nash thought at the time.

Scott Gradin had looked forward to Steve's visit. It was nice to finally meet the person he had spent so much time talking with on the phone during the past few months. He felt as if he had known Steve for years. In fact, by now, the Bronco assistant knew the entire Nash family, even their dog Quincy, on a first-name basis.

But what struck Gradin as he met Steve in person was his charisma. The campus visit had barely begun and already Steve Nash had other players gravitating towards him. Besides the obvious basketball skills he possessed, Steve was a born leader, a guy people wanted to be around. It was nice for Gradin to see he had been so right about this Canadian kid.

Meanwhile, on the inside, Steve felt a little intimidated during the visit. Here he was a Canadian high schooler hanging around with a group of what he considered to be fairly big-time U.S. college athletes. And a few of the veteran players on the Broncos seemed as if the last thing they wanted to do was to help him feel at home.

The basketball court provided the most pleasant surprise of the visit, as Steve got his first taste of playing ball with future teammates John Woolery and DeWayne Lewis, a pair of quick black guards from Los Angeles. "Geez, I don't get to play against guys this good all the time," Steve

Jason Sedlock took his recruiting visit to Santa Clara at the same time as Steve. Throughout their four seasons together, the two would become roommates and close friends.

thought. "And this is supposed to be a bad school?"

During the last couple of hours of his recruiting visit, Scott Gradin took him for a drive around the campus and the surrounding area. "I see a good marriage here between Santa Clara and Steve Nash," Gradin smiled.

In the end, after discussing things with his family, everybody agreed that Steve should go to Santa Clara. It was best.

Steve felt somewhat relieved that it was finally over. It had been a long time coming. Santa Clara wasn't Indiana, it wasn't Duke. But it was an NCAA Division One school offering him a full basketball scholarship. It was a chance for Steve to continue his dream and his parents liked the fact that all but three Santa Clara players in the past 22 years had earned a degree. There really hadn't been much of a decision to be made.

On April 13, 1992 — six days into basketball's spring signing period and just a day after returning from his recruiting visit to Santa Clara — Steve made it official. He was finally bound for the NCAA.

Not long after that, Bronco head coach Carroll Williams found himself in the living room of John and Jean Nash's suburban Victoria home. Despite the fact that Steve had already signed his letter of intent, Williams wanted to meet the Nash family and assure the parents that Santa Clara would be the right opportunity for their son.

The veteran Santa Clara coach fell in love with the Nash family almost immediately after arriving for the controlled home visit that NCAA recruiting regulations allow. Williams appreciated the warm environment of the Nash household, in which even a stranger felt comfortable right away. He liked the way brother Martin and sister Joann were genuinely excited for Steve. "He comes from good stock," Williams thought to himself.

John and Jean Nash, and their children Martin, Steve and Joann. The Santa Clara recruiting team was impressed by the warmth of the Nash family, and the support that they all offered to Steve. His family, especially his parents, continue to play a big role in Steve's life.

The Broncos coach enjoyed a home-cooked meal and the warm conversation around the Nash dinner table. He showed the family a video of a Santa Clara-San Francisco game from the just-completed season, as well as an informational video about the Santa Clara campus.

Williams also handed out brochures and literature on his school and explained the intricacies of an NCAA athletic scholarship. Later in the three-hour visit he met Ian Hyde-Lay, who had popped over from SMUS for the occasion.

Carroll Williams left the Nash house that night with a good feeling. As he drove back to the hotel, there was no doubt in the Santa Clara head coach's mind. His assistants had been right about this kid. The Broncos had landed themselves a good one.

The Steve Nash recruiting story would eventually turn into one of the most repeated sagas in college basketball during his senior year at Santa Clara. But the most interesting twist on the tale probably came courtesy of the Seattle *Post-Intelligencer*.

A feature by *Post-Intelligencer* writer Bud Withers in November of 1995 took the Washington Huskies to task for not so much as looking at Nash when he played high school ball only a 50-minute plane trip away. Withers noted somewhat sarcastically that the Huskies had also been looking for a point guard back in 1992, but had filled their opening with Prentiss Perkins, a junior college transfer from Minneapolis.

As Nash began his senior year at Santa Clara, Withers pointed out that Prentiss Perkins was languishing in a state prison in St. Cloud, Minnesota, scheduled to do time until May of 1998 on drug and assault convictions.

"I feel bad that people have been pointing that out," Steve would later say. "That guy's going to be pissed off at me when he gets out of the slammer."

So why did nearly every U.S. school pass on the chance to recruit Steve Nash? Why, to this day, does he have a shoebox full of rejection letters in a closet in his parent's house?

Well, it certainly wasn't a case of Nash not having the tools. Instead, it was likely more a matter of innocent, inbred basketball prejudice.

Canada has never been known as much of an exporter of basketball talent, let alone as a producer of point guards capable of starring in the NCAA. Most of the country's hoop exports have been what you would call raw material — seven-footers with limited skills being the stereotype — and too many of them over the years have been chewed up in the unforgiving machinery of big-time U.S. college basketball.

Race also likely played at least a small role in the Steve Nash recruiting story. It seems clear that white players are often regarded as inferior athletes by scouts and coaches. It wasn't by accident that Hollywood produced a movie called "White Men Can't Jump".

"When you're at Pepperdine you get, oh, 300 letters a year [from players looking for scholarships]. And for a white guard from Canada, you're probably not going to do a lot of follow-up," former Pepperdine coach Tom Asbury would later succinctly sum things up for the Los Angeles

Times as Steve's story made the rounds.

As his college career flourished, big-time coaches from time to time would bemoan the fact they hadn't recruited Steve Nash when they had the chance. Utah's Rick Majerus, who had been tipped off to Steve by national team coach Ken Shields, was quick to admit that he had made a mistake. Maryland coach Gary Williams, when it was pointed out that Nash's coach had written his program, asking for a scholarship, joked during the 1996 NCAA Tournament about his "damn assistants."

Long Beach State coach Seth Greenberg, who after some initial nibbling opted not to pursue Nash, ran into Steve at the 1995 Western Regional of the NCAA Tournament at Boise, Idaho. Greenberg wrapped Nash in a big bear hug: "This is the little twerp that made me look bad," he smiled.

Thinking back to Steve's Las Vegas experience, Ian Hyde-Lay believes many of the college scouts who frequent the summer prep tournament meat markets should beat the bushes a little harder. "The games they need to go to at these tournaments are the 9 a.m. specials on Saturday mornings," Hyde-Lay said. "That's when you really find out about the guy you're recruiting. Is he out there working his butt off in a game that's for fifth- and eighth-place? Is he a guy who loves to play?"

"All I know," Hyde-Lay added with a smile, "is that Scott Gradin should be in the Santa Clara Hall of Fame."

Since Steve Nash's story has come to light, U.S. coaches are likely more inclined to check out hot

A persistent Ian Hyde-Lay played a major role in finding Steve Nash a home with a Division One NCAA team.

B.C. prospects. Dick Davey, for one, now looks at enough Canadian footage every year that he could probably qualify for an honorary spot on the National Film Board. And it is doubtful that another player such as Nash will be so universally overlooked by all of the bigger U.S. schools.

In fact, Salmon Arm point guard Jordie McTavish, who has been compared more closely to Nash than any player to come out of B.C. since, was signed early by Rick Majerus for his Utah program. McTavish was scheduled to enter his freshman season in a Utes uniform at the same time Nash entered the NBA.

Simply put, the fact that Steve Nash ended up at Santa Clara, rather than at a major school such as Indiana, UCLA or North Carolina, was the result of a combination of circumstance and fate.

"It wasn't a case of being Einstein," Dick Davey would later admit to *Sports Illustrated*. "There was no magic wand. I just got very lucky."

Chapter Five

SETTLING IN AT SANTA CLARA

It was a morning just like every other morning for the past couple of weeks.

Steve Nash opened his eyes, lifted his head off the pillow, took a look around the small Santa Clara University dorm room he shared with fellow freshman Jason Sedlock — and desperately wished that he was somewhere else.

It was mid-November of 1992. And another morning meant another day. Another day meant another basketball practice with Dick Davey.

Davey had recruited Steve in Vancouver just eight months earlier and become the Broncos' new head coach after the September move of Carroll Williams into the SCU athletic director's chair. And Dick Davey's coaching style was not about mollycoddling his players. Particularly when it came to a certain freshman named Steve Nash.

Things had actually started out alright for Steve at the Bay Area private school. He had arrived on campus about a month before classes began to get a head start on the basketball court. And initially he'd been excited about being away from home and enrolled in this picturesque university, with its palm trees, quaint monastery-style buildings and distinctly Californian flavor.

Dick Davey had been tough on Steve from the onset of practice in late October, however. And Steve certainly found the level of basketball competition much faster, stronger and more competitive than what he'd been used to in the past. Nevertheless, considering he was a freshman from Canada, he had more than held his own and even dominated during stretches of some early scrimmages.

But things had taken a decided turn for the worse in early November after Steve came down with a severe case of the flu. He became so sick and dehydrated that he had to be hospitalized overnight and placed on an IV.

By the time he returned to practice a few days later, he was much weaker than normal. Now, the competition from veteran point guard John Woolery that had been all he could handle before the illness was suddenly too much for Steve. He was being pushed off the ball, manhandled defensively. And worst of all, he was often being picked clean by the cat-quick Woolery.

If there had been one area of his game Steve always had utmost confidence in, it was his ballhandling. Now he was having trouble just getting the ball upcourt against the aggressive Woolery, a junior from Los Angeles Fairfax High School with long arms, quick feet and plenty of defensive smarts. And if Steve wasn't having the ball stolen outright, he was watching as his passes into the post were being tipped away and cashed in for dunks at the other end.

To Nash's new teammates, it was no big deal. Most of them knew by now that John Woolery was a vastly underrated defender and just one of those guys you hated to play against, anytime. But for a player such as Steve who prided himself on his ballhandling, it was humiliating to have somebody steal his rock over and over again.

It was the most discouraging time Steve had ever experienced in sports. Having the ball continuously stolen made him feel naked out there on the practice floor, like he had nothing.

During these few weeks, Steve had begun to doubt his own abilities — something that had never happened before. Why was he playing this game, he wondered, when he couldn't handle a

Division One guard who wasn't even all-conference? If he couldn't function here, how would he ever reach the level he dreamed of?

What Steve Nash was unaware of, however, was just how tough John Woolery was. Woolery didn't get much hype as an NCAA point guard, mainly because he wasn't a particularly good shooter and because he played at a small university. But few other point guards in the country would have looked forward to bringing the ball up against him. Woolery had come out of a terrific Los Angeles Fairfax high school program that had produced the likes of NBAers Sean Higgins and Chris Mills. He could play, and more than just a little.

Woolery, who had become the leader of the Broncos as his junior season approached, wasn't too worried about the trials of Steve Nash, even through these shaky November days. He had been impressed with this Canadian kid since the day Nash had arrived the previous spring for his recruiting visit. Woolery could immediately tell by the way Steve handled the ball that he was going to be good. But more than that, Woolery liked the way Steve asked questions. This kid wanted so much to be better. And that was something John Woolery could respect.

Still, Woolery wasn't exactly surprised, either, as Steve struggled through practice after practice. He was just a freshman, and this was a huge step up from high school. It would take time for this kid from Canada to get his feet under him, just like everybody else.

Even as Woolery constantly harassed Steve during practice, hounding him on the dribble and tipping away his passes, he did it with the idea of making his new teammate better. He knew the freshman would be his partner down the road, and he wanted to make him as tough as possible.

John Woolery believed Steve Nash could take it, too. He might get frustrated, but he always bounced back. And if you made a suggestion to him, the freshman always seemed to return a few days later with that advice already put to good use.

The other thing that had instantly struck Woolery about this Canadian newcomer was his work ethic. Despite Steve's obvious frustrations, he was there at Toso Pavilion alone before practice, after practice, and often during extra sessions that extended well past midnight. "He works harder than anybody I've ever played with, by far," Woolery thought.

But all that hard work seemed to be going for naught as far as Steve was concerned. He was having trouble accomplishing even the most fundamental tasks on the court. And to compound matters, Dick Davey was constantly yelling at him in practice. Things seemed to be getting worse instead of better.

On this particular morning, as he glanced groggily around his spartan SCU dorm room, with its matching bunks and twin desks, Steve literally ached to be back in Victoria. He missed his family, his friends and his dog.

He was also consumed by a sudden dread of the practice floor. Basketball practice had always been something Steve looked forward to. But these days it had mutated into a miserable chore. Steve thought about it at lunch, in class, when he was walking to and from his dorm room. Basketball just wasn't much fun right now.

Santa Clara coach Dick Davey shouts out directions to his Broncos from the sidelines. Davey and Nash had a fiery relationship.

Everything about Santa Clara practices seemed so tense and negative, an atmosphere different than anything Steve had experienced while playing for Ian Hyde-Lay back at SMUS. But this wasn't high school ball up in Canada anymore. It was NCAA Division One, where coaches can sometimes lose their jobs for losing games. And that pressure, Steve was finding out quickly, was passed on to the players well before each college season even started.

To Steve, Dick Davey seemed much different than the man who had recruited him at the B.C. high school tournament in the Agrodome back in March. Davey, a 15-year assistant at Santa Clara who was now getting his chance at the head job, wasn't an easy man to please on the practice floor.

Steve really wanted to go home. But he couldn't. If he went home, he'd be a quitter. And if he went home, he'd have let Dick Davey beat him.

From Dick Davey's perspective, there was absolutely no reason that Steve Nash, with his obvious skills, couldn't step in right away and contribute at Santa Clara. He believed Nash had the potential to play beyond the college level and his job was to draw that potential out. His philosophy was to be tough on his players in order to make them tougher when tip-off rolled around.

When his freshman guard began to struggle as the Broncos' season approached, Davey didn't worry right away. He knew that John Woolery, if not the best defender he'd ever seen at Santa Clara, was certainly in the top two or three. Woolery had that combination of long arms, quickness, intelligence and feel for the game that could quickly eliminate options for any opponent. It was only natural Woolery would give a freshman some problems.

But when this particular freshman continued to flounder through early November, a tiny voice inside Davey began to wonder. Small cracks of

doubt began to break across the veteran coach's mind. Maybe, just maybe, he had overrated this Canadian kid.

Truthfully, Davey hadn't expected Steve Nash to struggle at all. He had assumed that Steve would step in and be a player right away with little or no problem. From the day he had first laid eyes on Steve in person, Davey had pegged him as a major diamond in the rough, a player who was going to make a tremendous impact on the Broncos' program. He was a little surprised and disappointed that this Canadian kid wasn't able to do it right away.

Every time Steve would fail in some small way, Dick Davey was discouraged with him. He expected complete efficiency from the freshman and, when he didn't get it, he let Steve know that he was unhappy. And he let him know loudly.

Still, Davey managed to remain fairly positive that Steve Nash would turn the corner sometime soon. And besides, the Santa Clara coach comforted himself, Nash wouldn't have to play against John Woolery once the real games began.

Right from Steve Nash's first day on campus, Scott Gradin made a point of keeping an eye on his prize recruit.

Gradin, the young assistant who had been most responsible for bringing the Canadian south, wasn't too worried about Steve's performance in practice. He knew the youngster was frustrated but he also knew that this was a rite of passage that nearly every college player goes through. Gradin was determined to help Steve weather the rough spots and handle the weight of Dick Davey's expectations. He was always there to talk or to put an encouraging arm around the young freshman's shoulder after a tough practice.

Steve made his NCAA debut by going one-for-one from the field in limited floor time during a 71-56 road win at San Jose State. Four days later, he was unmistakably nervous as he came off the bench in UCLA's historic Pauley Pavilion. In the ensuing minutes, he missed three relatively easy shots — a couple of them rather bad misses — and he also committed a pair of turnovers before being pulled by Davey. Steve returned to the bench clearly disappointed as the Broncos would go on to lose to the Bruins by a 69-60 margin.

Gradin moved down the bench to console the freshman. "Three years from now," he calmly spoke into Steve's ear after the player had sat down, "the difference will be that you'll be three-for-three from the floor with three assists during that same stretch."

As it turned out, Steve wouldn't have to wait three years for his big break in the Broncos' program. It came just six games later, when John Woolery went down with an injury.

Woolery had to undergo arthroscopic surgery on his left knee, an injury which would keep him out of the lineup for three games. And despite the problems Steve had shown early on in practice, Dick Davey started him at the point during that stretch.

Steve made the most of the opportunity, particularly in his first start against the Minnesota Gophers at Toso Pavilion. The Broncos lost the game 87-63 but Steve scored a team-high 15 points on three-for-four shooting from behind

After some early struggles at Santa Clara, Steve Nash bounced back with confidence to end his freshman season strongly.

the arc. More importantly, he didn't make a single turnover in 27 minutes of court time.

Steve was thrilled. His confidence had returned and he felt he'd made a significant breakthrough. But obviously, he was not yet a household name, at least not as far as the San Francisco *Chronicle* was concerned.

"John Nash, a freshman point guard who scored 15 points in his first collegiate start …" the newspaper's game story read.

The mistake couldn't have mattered less to Steve, however. Prior to the Minnesota game, he had averaged 3.9 points and 14.5 minutes during the Broncos' first seven contests. The Minnesota game meant he had finally arrived.

After that breakthrough, Steve saw lots of time for a freshman. Once Woolery returned to the point, Dick Davey knew he had to find Steve some minutes elsewhere. They came at the off-guard spot, where Steve's three-point touch proved to be the missing ingredient the Broncos needed. After averaging just 5.8 points in Santa Clara's first 16 games, Nash would post 11.3 per game during the next 11. The time at the off-guard spot helped him to feel much more comfortable when it came time to spell John Woolery at the point.

During the final third of the season, Steve averaged nearly 30 minutes a game — mostly at the two spot — and led the team in scoring. By the end of the regular season, he had started five games and averaged 24 minutes per game for the entire schedule. He would eventually finish fourth in team scoring for the season at 8.1 points per game, post 12 games in double figures and drain 49 three-pointers, an SCU freshman record. His 252 points for the season would be the most for a Santa Clara rookie since 1978.

"I think if we'd opened up the offence for him, we'd have gotten earlier results," Dick Davey told the San Jose *Mercury News* late that season. "I'm not saying he's a pro, but he's real good. He almost has the ability to play anywhere in the country."

As the WCC regular season came to a close, Steve had progressed to the point where he was a major contributor for the Broncos. Practices were often an exercise in humiliation, but the games were fun. He was getting yelled at consistently, but he was getting a chance to play.

But the excitement of playing was tempered by a continually confusing relationship with head coach Dick Davey, whose attitude toward Steve had definitely not softened. Publicly, and with the media, Davey was known as a jovial, gentle man always ready with a quick wit and a good quote. But like any coach, he could be tough on his team. And Steve Nash often felt Davey was particularly tough on him.

At half-time of a road game against the University of San Francisco near the end of his freshman season, the problem escalated.

During the game's first 20 minutes, Steve felt he had played well, missing just one shot. But Davey came into the locker room at half-time and ripped into him viciously for allowing passes to go into the post.

Steve was stunned. He didn't remember letting a single pass get into the post in the entire half. Was Davey making some kind of mental challenge to him? It was the only explanation he could think of.

Steve offered no reaction as the coach dressed him down in front of his teammates. Davey, obviously interpreting this as a sign of dissent, screamed at Steve: "If you don't like it, you can take your ass back to Canada!"

These were confusing times for Steve. But things were made much more palatable by the success the Broncos were now enjoying on the court. With Steve playing a valuable role, SCU had won six of its last seven games to close out the regular season. Heading into the West Coast Conference playoff tournament at the University of San

Francisco's tradition-laden Memorial Gymnasium, the Broncos were on a roll.

They continued that roll at USF, downing archrival Saint Mary's College 79-68 and Gonzaga 53-51 to advance to the tournament final. Now the Broncos, a group that had been picked by some to finish last in the conference, were just one win away from the WCC playoff title and an automatic berth in the NCAA Tournament.

All of this was a little difficult for Steve Nash to grasp. After a Fall in which things had at times seemed so hopeless, here he was just one win away from joining college basketball's Big Dance.

Despite their sudden success, the Broncos were still considered the underdogs heading into the Monday-night WCC tournament final against the Pepperdine Waves, the top-ranked team in the conference with 22 wins and the heavy favourite to emerge from the WCC into the NCAA's 64-team extravaganza. And as the game unfolded live on an ESPN national broadcast, that seemed to be the way things would play out.

The Waves rolled out to a 19-5 lead in the first half, at one stage running off 14 straight points. Santa Clara, meanwhile, got off to a horrible start, shooting only 35 per cent from the field and pulling down just seven rebounds in total.

But during the second half, Santa Clara would go on to stage one of the most deadly three-point shooting exhibitions in NCAA history. And leading the way would be a slender freshman named Steve Nash.

After scoring just three points in the opening 20 minutes, Steve took complete control in the second half. He nailed an immediate three, drove for a hoop and then, with an untied shoelace flopping about, drained another three. Suddenly the Broncos were within only four points of Pepperdine with 13:40 remaining.

Steve had scored the first seven points of the half to jumpstart the SCU offence. The revitalized Broncos would go on to connect on all nine of their long-distance attempts during the second half — with Steve hitting four of those — to eventually post a 73-63 shocker in front of 4,029 wildly pro-Santa Clara fans.

"It's not really complicated," a stunned Pepperdine coach Tom Asbury told the *Chronicle* afterward. "They just hit every big shot."

Steve Nash had hit the biggest ones, finishing the game with a career-high 23 points on five-for-six shooting from the three-point range. A few minutes after the final buzzer rang, he became the first freshman ever to win WCC playoff tournament MVP honors. But more important to this ecstatic teenager from Canada, the Santa Clara Broncos were going to their first NCAA Tournament since 1987. Steve was actually going to be a part of the event that he had always dreamed about.

The persona of Steve Nash, the college basketball star, was officially born on this steamy night at USF. Ecstatic fans carried signs that read: "We are NASH-TY". Steve had continually urged the crowd to its feet during the dying minutes as the Broncos salted away the victory. And after the final buzzer, many of those fans hoisted him onto their shoulders. It was the kind of scene

Steve Nash's exceptional three-point touch would come in handy for the Broncos throughout his career at Santa Clara.

Steve had pictured during all those hours spent alone shooting a basketball.

"Steve's got great heart," Santa Clara teammate Mark Schmitz told the *Chronicle*. "When he started hitting shots and playing to the crowd, it got us on a roll."

None of the Broncos had been on a bigger roll than Nash, however. He had transformed himself from a freshman who didn't want to take too many shots for fear of alienating his older teammates to a guy who wanted the ball during crunch time. After going zero-for-seven from three-point range at rival Saint Mary's on February 26, Nash had gone on an incredible three-point binge of 15-for-19 during the next four games with the Broncos' season hanging in the balance. That clutch performance had certainly not gone unnoticed.

"These are high-pressure

Balancing his early struggles at Santa Clara were some awfully sweet victories for Steve Nash.

games with a lot at stake. And for an 18-year-old freshman to be doing that well under this kind of pressure ... I think we're seeing something very unique," former Laker and UCLA great Kareem Abdul-Jabbar, an analyst for ESPN, observed during the national broadcast of the WCC Tournament final.

Before the cameras had clicked off completely following his first-ever ESPN interview, Steve even managed to slip in a quick: "What's up, Victoria!"

"I just felt it tonight," Steve would later tell the San Francisco *Examiner*. "I knew I could miss those shots I took, but it just helped me focus better. It was a chance to give us the big lift."

The victory was a major surprise to followers of college basketball in the Bay Area. The Broncos, who had graduated four starters from the previous season, had been tabbed to finish seventh in their league. This was the same team that had shot just 16.4 per cent in an embarrassing loss to Stanford earlier in the season. The *Examiner*'s Frank Blackman wrote: "Santa Clara in the NCAA Tournament? Get serious."

Serious was a good word to describe the Broncos' recent three-point roll. All told, they had hit 34 of 59 long-distance attempts during their past four games with their excitable Canadian freshman leading the long-distance assault.

Certainly, the Broncos had made a major turnaround from the struggling team that had been 5-6 and 9-10 earlier in the season. But it had been a particularly unbelievable about-face for Nash, who suddenly found himself getting the kind of treatment reserved for major stars.

Examiner sports columnist Ray Ratto penned a major post-tournament piece, headlined: "Nash proves dreams do come true." In it, Ratto described Steve as a "militantly self-effacing freshman and the non-hockey-playing pride of Victoria, British Columbia."

"If someone had asked Pepperdine coach Tom Asbury about the Canadian national anthem, he'd have said, 'Oh Canada, Why don't you keep your kids at home?'," Ratto wrote. Later, he concluded the same column by writing: " 'Oh Canada.' It's a damned catchy tune."

Under the headline: "Freshman's story better than fiction," *Mercury News* college basketball writer John Akers asked: "Who cloned Bobby Hurley and sent him to Santa Clara?"

It was an amazing transformation for Steve Nash. "I started the year and I was questioning whether I should even be playing the game," he thought. "But I fought through it.'

"Everything I had hoped and dreamed for has come true," Steve told the *Mercury News* in a pre-NCAA Tournament article. "Now I'll have to hope and dream for bigger things."

The sobering news following Santa Clara's huge victory over Pepperdine was the Broncos had drawn the mighty Arizona Wildcats for their opening game of the NCAA West Regional less than two weeks later in Salt Lake City. Tiny Santa Clara was entering the game as the region's number 15 seed. The Broncos were given virtually no chance against Arizona, the number two seed in the West and the fifth seed overall in the tournament.

The Broncos entered the tournament with a respectable 18-11 record, but history was against them. Only once before had a fifteenth seed knocked off a number two. In fact, the number 15 seeds had compiled a pitiful 1-33 record in first-round NCAA Tournament match-ups.

Under their white-haired, majestic coach Lute Olson, the Wildcats were entering the game with a 24-3 record and what many considered to be a great shot at going all the way to the Final Four in New Orleans. Arizona had gone 17-1 to win the Pac-10 conference title. By comparison, the Broncos had fallen by 31 points to Stanford, who had finished in the Pac-10 basement at 2-16.

This Arizona lineup was incredibly deep and talented. It featured three future NBAers, with Damon Stoudamire and Khalid Reeves in the backcourt and Chris Mills at small forward, as well as seven-foot centre Ed Stokes inside. The Broncos, who had been led recently by a skinny freshman from Canada, boasted six-foot-nine forward Pete Eisenrich as their biggest player.

"Our chances are not good," Dick Davey told the Salt Lake *Tribune* on the eve of the tournament. "We talked to our players about that. We don't want to kid anyone. We're going to need to play a close to perfect game to have a chance. At the same time, that's not something that can't be done."

"As soon as we made it [the Tournament], we changed our goals," Steve Nash added in the same article.

Lute Olson's Arizona team, meanwhile, seemed determined not to take the Broncos lightly. Just a year earlier, the Wildcats had been upset 87-80 by fourteenth-seed East Tennessee State in the NCAA Tournament's opening round. Arizona players were certain they would not let that happen again.

"We're thinking about that game against East Tennessee State last year," Stoudamire told the *Tribune*. "We were overconfident and didn't give East Tennessee State that much credit. We can't overlook anyone."

The Broncos were raring to go as they approached the 6:04 p.m. tip-off time in the Huntsman Center. So were their fans. Santa Clara

had averaged only 2,700 spectators that season back at Toso Pavilion, yet plenty of alumni and students had scrambled to get to Salt Lake City for this game, the Broncos' first NCAA Tournament appearance in six years. Once they got there, these fans were determined to make the most of the experience, too, dressing in Bronco maroon and carrying a variety of imaginative signs, including one that read: "Do it for Rambis," a reference to Santa Clara's most famous basketball alumnus.

"I'm so excited, I can't wait" Dick Davey said in the *Tribune*'s pre-game story "But at 6:30, you might see me sagging. We might have trouble because we'll be nervous. If we don't stay close in the first ten minutes, it could be an ugly game."

That was Davey's public stance. But just before his team took to the court, with 11,739 fans waiting in the stands and millions more watching on national television, the Santa Clara coach told his players: "Outside of this locker room, I don't think anybody out there thinks we can do it. But I know we can."

The Broncos began the game as if they believed their coach, outworking the Wildcats defensively and on the boards and taking a stunning 12-point lead 15 minutes into the first half. But mighty Arizona recovered to score 25 straight points during the next ten minutes. And when Chris Mills scored with 15:26 left to give the Wildcats a 46-33 lead, the dance appeared to be all over for Cinderella Santa Clara.

But that's when the collars began to get tight for Arizona and the juices started flowing for the Broncos. Mills picked up his fourth foul just 15 seconds later and was forced to the bench for ten minutes. The Arizona star would finish with 19 points but, more importantly, he would be on the bench for the decisive stages of the game.

With Mills out, the Broncos began their unlikely climb back into contention, grabbing just about every rebound and loose ball and harassing Arizona's shaky shooters. Santa Clara junior forward Pete Eisenrich, who prior to the game had told the *Chronicle* that beating Arizona would be like winning the national championship for the Broncos, had the most to do with making it happen, scoring 19 points, including the go-ahead jumper with 2:40 left that gave Santa Clara the lead for good.

Steve Nash played a huge role for the Broncos down the stretch. As Arizona desperately fouled to try to stop the clock in the final minute, the Canadian freshman was the direct beneficiary.

During the game's final 31 seconds, with the basketball world watching breathlessly, Steve would make six straight free throws to ice the biggest win in SCU basketball history. It was a scene that would become forever linked with the Nash name as he ran each time from the backcourt straight to the foul line, eager to make each one of those monumental free throws.

But just as the CBS commentators were raving about the ice-water running through this young Canadian's veins, Steve showed some freshman nerves. After hitting six straight free throws to give the Broncos a 64-61 lead, Steve finally missed a pair with 7.3 seconds left.

His second miss was rebounded by fellow SCU freshman Kevin Dunne, who was immediately fouled. But with 5.1 seconds remaining, Dunne also missed both ends at the line.

The Wildcats had one last desperate chance to avoid this colossal upset. Damon Stoudamire sped the ball up the floor and launched an off-balance three-pointer. But as the buzzer sounded, the ball clanged off the rim. The Wildcats were out. Santa Clara had pulled off one of the biggest upsets in NCAA Tournament history.

"Obviously, there was a lot of pressure in that situation," Steve would later say about those monumental free throws. "But if you want to be a basketball player at this level, those are the kind of moments you have to enjoy. All my life, I've wanted to be in that situation and I'm glad I didn't run from it."

Steve finished the game with ten points and his free throws had been instrumental in the victory. But the biggest Santa Clara factor had likely come on the boards, where tiny SCU had grabbed a staggering 50 rebounds, compared to 36 for much bigger Arizona.

"They didn't panic. I did, but they didn't." Broncos coach Dick Davey would tell *USA Today* of his team after it was over.

The upset caused headlines across the basketball world. *USA Today* declared: "Santa Clara pulls 64-61 stunner". The Washington *Post* ran with: "Santa Clara, 15th Seed, Razes Arizona".

The loss turned up the heat on Arizona coach Lute Olson, whose powerful team had been upset for the second straight spring. "I don't feel jinxed," Olson told the Chicago *Tribune*. "Just frustrated that we couldn't play the way we were capable of playing."

Two days later, the Broncos' incredible spring run would come to a quick end, as they ran into a ferociously defensive Temple Owls lineup that included future NBAers Aaron McKie and Eddie Jones. Santa Clara was simply outmatched athletically and, after their triumph over Arizona, there was no way they were sneaking up on intense Owls coach John Chaney and his famous Temple zone.

The Broncos bowed out of the tournament with a 68-57 loss. But nobody would forget about them on The Road to New Orleans. And Steve Nash would certainly never forget the experience, either.

"It was incredible to be part of something you had always watched before from the outside," he said a couple of weeks after the Arizona game. "I have been watching this tournament since the seventh grade. But this year, it's different because I was there. I came out of the tunnel in my uniform and saw 11,000 people cheering and all the TV cameras and the bands and I said: 'This is college basketball.'

"It felt great."

Sometimes it is difficult to live up to expectations. The Broncos could have asked Arizona all about that. But they would find out soon enough for themselves during Steve Nash's sophomore year at SCU.

Much was expected of the Broncos with four starters returning from their unlikely Tournament team of 1992-93, but success simply didn't materialize as head coach Dick Davey, Steve Nash and the Broncos were hit by a touch of the sophomore jinx.

The Broncos would finish the 1993-94 season with a disappointing 13-14 overall record. And any hopes of making up for that with another dramatic run through the post-season were dashed when Santa Clara opened the 1994 WCC tournament at Toso with a 76-74 loss to the University of San Francisco.

In terms of statistics, it would turn out to be a solid season for Steve as he started 23 of 26 games and averaged better than 29 minutes a game. He also averaged 14.6 points, mostly from the two-guard spot, becoming the first sophomore in seven seasons to lead the Broncos in scoring. Steve also set new Santa Clara records with 67 three-pointers made and 168 attempted, shooting 40 per cent from behind the arc.

Steve had got off to a sizzling start, hitting double figures in the Broncos' first seven games and averaging 18 points during that stretch. But an Achilles strain led to a mid-season slump in which he scored better than ten points just twice over a ten-game span. During the last nine games of the season, Steve would set the tone for his junior and senior years by averaging 18.5 points and shooting 47.4 per cent from the field.

There had certainly been enough highlights to make most college sophomores happy. Steve scored a career-high 29 points against Pac-10 school Oregon and turned in a strong 16-point effort in an exhibition against Arizona and Damon Stoudamire. The Wildcats, on their way to a Final Four appearance, exacted a small measure of revenge for the previous spring with an 89-63 rout of the Broncos at San Jose Arena.

Perhaps the most impressive result of the sophomore season had been an 80-67 December win over the 13th-ranked California Bears and

Sophomore Steve Nash more than held his own against NBA-bound Jason Kidd during an 80-67 Broncos' win.

their superstar point guard Jason Kidd at the Oakland Coliseum. It was considered to be a major upset for the unranked Broncos as this Cal team included another future NBAer in Lamond Murray. Steve stepped up in that game, too, scoring 17 points on three-for-four shooting from three-point range, grabbing seven rebounds and adding three steals and four assists. Perhaps as important, Steve had a big part in holding Jason Kidd to just 14 points.

Talk had already started to circulate about Steve Nash being a possible NBA prospect. Opposing

coaches had begun to laud him, including Cal coach Todd Bozeman, who described Steve as "a budding John Stockton".

But while other coaches appreciated Steve Nash, he didn't always feel Dick Davey shared those sentiments. Their relationship continued to be somewhat strained through this sophomore season, especially with the Broncos on their way to a losing record.

Things reached a head during a three-point league loss at Portland in late January. Steve had made his first three three-point attempts, but Davey didn't appreciate what he perceived to be a poor attitude on the part of the sophomore guard during the game's early stages. After Steve missed on his next three-point try, Davey chased down the sideline and yelled at him: "What the hell? Focus! How can you miss that shot? You had zero focus!"

Steve was shocked. "Nobody in the history of the game has made all their threes," he thought. "I'm three-for-four. I miss one and all of a sudden I have zero focus? What? Did I try to miss it?"

Steve was clearly frustrated and his face showed it. Immediately, he was yanked from the game by Davey. Then things got worse. The Santa Clara coach strode down to the end of the bench. "Oh, tough now? You're a tough guy, aren't you?" he said to Steve.

"What?" Steve replied. "I missed a shot."

"OK, so you want to talk back now ..." Davey yelled.

The coach walked back toward his seat on the bench. A stunned Steve looked straight ahead at the game continuing out on the court. He didn't say a word or even change his expression.

Davey obviously thought differently. He turned around in mid-stride and yelled: "What? Oh, you've got something to say? OK that's pretty cool. OK tough guy …"

Davey was as angry as he had ever been on the sidelines. It wasn't the missed shot but rather the questionable attitude he felt he was seeing on the part of Steve Nash.

Inside, Steve was fuming just as much. He didn't understand why Davey was so upset with him. "I don't need this," he thought. "I work my butt off harder than anybody on the team, probably in the conference. I don't deserve this. Especially when I'm playing great."

Not long after that incident, Dick Davey approached Steve following a practice at Toso. "What's wrong? You don't seem like yourself," the coach said.

"Well, to be honest with you, I'm not having any fun," Steve replied. "It's no fun at all. You're really negative. I don't think it's good for the team and I'm not enjoying myself. I'd love to go play basketball in the park every day, but I don't like coming here every day."

Davey used this opportunity to get something off his chest, too. He said he felt that Steve had been doing a lot of complaining on the court and he told his star guard that he should concentrate on keeping his emotions under better control.

Steve felt that this talk resulted in a change in Dick Davey. The coach became more positive for the remainder of his sophomore season. The Broncos really didn't turn things around record-wise, but it was a much more constructive atmosphere at Toso as the season concluded.

His curious relationship with Dick Davey,

Like any coach, Dick Davey could be tough on his team. His high expectations made life especially hard for Steve Nash.

combined with the limitations of the Broncos basketball program, caused Steve to do some serious soul-searching after his sophomore year ended at Santa Clara. He was now getting some unofficial feelers from people about the possibility of transferring out of the Bronco program, to a bigger school with more TV coverage. And he was wondering what it would be like to play under a different coach.

Steve felt that Utah, under high-profile head coach Rick Majerus, was one place he might enjoy playing. Kentucky was another. These kinds of programs, Steve was pretty sure, would afford him better opportunities to make it to the NBA.

Davey was aware of the outside influences on his star player during this period. He knew people were telling Steve that he was "better than that", that he should look to transfer. Davey decided to open the door for the sophomore guard.

The Broncos head coach told Steve he didn't want him at Santa Clara if Steve honestly felt there was another situation he wanted more or one he thought would be better for him. "You make the decision," Davey told Steve. "If you want to go, it's your choice. I don't want people here who don't want to be here."

In the end, Steve decided to stay put. After

giving the idea of transferring a great deal of thought, he decided that he could accomplish his goals at Santa Clara. Paramount in his decision was the fact that he didn't want to leave his teammates behind.

At Santa Clara, he also had a situation that was his. Transferring would bring a lot of unknowns. "I can do it here," he thought. "It's up to me, not up to the school."

The trials of sophomore year disappeared during Steve Nash's breakthrough junior season. It was a fine year, indeed, for Bronco basketball as Dick

Left to right, Steve Nash, Jason Sedlock, Phil Von Buchwaldt and Adam Anderson take a breather on the Santa Clara Broncos' bench. Despite interest from other schools and pressures to consider a transfer, Nash didn't want to leave his teammates behind.

Davey's team went 21-7 and his junior point guard emerged as a bonafide NBA prospect.

It was a season that would include so many highlights — a win over the Oregon Ducks at Toso in which Steve had 34 points and eight assists; a five-point December loss to the nationally fifth-ranked Jayhawks in Lawrence, Kansas, a game in which Steve had 20 points and five assists; and a 23-point, ten-assist showing in a 77-62 victory at Saint Mary's that clinched the Broncos' first regular-season title since 1970.

For Steve Nash individually, it couldn't have gone much better. He averaged 20.9 points and 6.4 assists to lead the WCC in both categories, a feat achieved by only an elite few including Utah Jazz great John Stockton. Steve also led the league in three-point percentage (.454, up five per cent from his sophomore season) and was among the NCAA's national Top ten in four separate offensive categories.

To top things off, Steve also became Santa Clara's first WCC player of the year since Kurt Rambis in 1980. He was a unanimous choice in voting by the league's coaches. Also a unanimous winner was Dick Davey as WCC coach of the year.

Although he had always been known in Canada as a point guard, Steve actually made a name for himself at that position in U.S. circles as a junior. With John Woolery lost to graduation, this was now clearly Steve's team to run. And run it he did, finishing the season with six ten-plus assist games. A recipient of many of his passes was fellow Victorian Brendan Graves, a six-foot-ten centre who had joined Steve in the Broncos lineup that year after transferring out of Cal following his sophomore season.

There were several big games for Steve Nash that winter, including Steve's WCC record 21-for-21 performance at the free-throw line against Saint Mary's and his memorable 40-point effort (35 in the second half and overtime) as the Broncos ended Gonzaga's 34-game homecourt winning streak with a dramatic 73-68 decision in Spokane.

"It took nearly three years to construct Gonzaga's homecourt winning streak," wrote Dave Bolig of the Spokane *Spokesman-Review* after that game. "Thirty-four wins, right on top of another, like bricks on an expanding wall. And it took all of 25 minutes by an uncanny Steve Nash of Santa Clara to topple it all."

That was just one of a glowing list of quotes on Steve Nash that grew as his junior season progressed. He was building hype like a snowball rolling down a hill on a spring day.

"Nash is a big-time player who will be playing in the NBA soon," proclaimed Saint Mary's head coach Ernie Kent.

"We tried to hold him in check, but it's an impossible task, really," San Diego coach and former UCLA guard Brad Holland told the *Mercury News* after a loss to Santa Clara. "Steve Nash is too good to hold for very long. He's a playmaker, yet he's a scorer. He can make plays, spoon-feed players for lay-ins and play defence. On top of that, he's a great leader. He's enriched their program tremendously. He'd be a very good guard in any league."

"The Broncos' Steve Nash is, barring injury or other calamity, an almost certain first-round selection in the 1996 NBA draft," wrote Frank Burlison of the Long Beach *Press-Telegram*.

Steve Nash signs an autograph for a fan — something which would occur with more and more frequency as his college career progressed.

The Broncos were full of confidence heading into the post-season of Steve Nash's junior year — and they had good reason for that confidence. They had gone 12-2 in the regular season, including a nine-game winning streak, and they were heavily favoured to win the WCC post-season tournament. To top things off, the tournament was being played in their own Toso Pavilion, where they had a perfect record.

Most folks expected the Broncos to cruise through the eight-team tournament and right into the NCAA's big show. But it didn't work out that way as Santa Clara and Steve Nash were stunned 87-83 by the Lions of Loyola Marymount in the first round. The giant-killers of the Silicon Valley had themselves been knocked off.

It was an embarrassing loss for Steve and his teammates as the Broncos became the first number one seed in the nine-year history of the WCC tournament to lose in the opening round.

The Broncos had enjoyed a 55-48 lead over Loyola Marymount with just under 13 minutes to play in the second half before things disintegrated in front of their home fans. The Lions, with absolutely nothing to lose, got red-hot from the field in the second half to pull away with the huge upset. Four LMU starters shot a combined 26-for-38 for the game. Steve finished the game with an impressive 20 points and nine assists but he had also committed seven turnovers.

"This will be tough to take," Steve told the San Jose *Mercury News*. "In 20 years, it'll still be tough to take. There was a lack of something, some sort of desire. There's no secret we can win that game."

Dick Davey, meanwhile, was disappointed and seemingly resigned to the fact that the Broncos would not be awarded an at-large berth in the NCAA Tournament. History seemed to back up the Bronco coach, too, since only two West Coast Conference teams had ever been given an at-large berth in the history of the NCAA Tournament.

"I'm proud of these kids and what they've done. But I don't think you should have rewards that aren't warranted and the way we played the last two weeks, I'm not sure they're warranted," Davey told the *Mercury News*. "We have to regroup and see if someone thinks we're worthy of going to the NIT."

Davey was referring to the National Invitational Tournament, which once was the dominant post-season college basketball event but now accepts the best teams which don't make it into the much more glamorous NCAA Tournament draw.

The Broncos' only remaining chance of making the preferred 64-team NCAA Tournament field was to receive an "at-large" bid. Each year, the tournament's selection committee awards a number of at-large berths in addition to the conference regular-season and playoff tournament champions which get automatic berths.

The Broncos had a couple of things going for them in the selection sweepstakes. They had posted a 20-7 record over a tough schedule, including the win over Oregon and the five-point loss to national power Kansas and they had dominated their conference during the regular season. They also carried a respectable RPI (Ratings Performance Index) of number 46. That

number signified where the Broncos were ranked according to a formula based on both how well a team performs and the strength of its schedule.

Still, not many people were giving the Broncos a chance heading into Selection Sunday, the day college basketball coaches, teams and fans gather in front of the television to watch both the draw and the at-large teams announced live.

Word of Santa Clara's selection reached Broncos' sports information director Jim Young and head coach Dick Davey about ten minutes before the announcement was made official on CBS. But Steve Nash and his teammates didn't find out until the words "Santa Clara" appeared on the screen. While highly-regarded teams such as Georgia Tech, George Washington and Texas Tech had been snubbed, the Broncos were going to the tournament. They would meet Mississippi State University in the first round that Friday in Boise, Idaho.

Before the name of Santa Clara's opponent had even been posted, Steve and housemates Kevin Dunne, Drew Zurek and Jason Sedlock were half-way around the block, having taken off in a mad victory dash. When they returned to their front yard, they dog-piled on each other wildly. Steve had been up since 7 a.m., scouring the lists of teams and analyzing the Broncos' chances of a berth, so when Santa Clara's name had been called, it had been a huge relief.

Certainly, the Broncos had backed their way into the tournament this time. The *Mercury News* referred to Santa Clara's bid as "stunningly unexpected". But Steve didn't care.

He was just happy to be going back to the Big Dance.

Heading into Boise a few days later, things didn't look particularly promising for the Broncos.

Steve was nursing a sore right ankle and suffering from a severe case of the flu, which had kept him out of practices in the past week. The Broncos were up against an athletic Mississippi State team which had already beaten Kentucky and defending national champion Arkansas that season and had the top-rated defence in the NCAA in terms of field-goal percentage allowed.

There was also absolutely no way the Broncos were going to surprise their first-round opponent this time, either.

"That part of the scenario and the so-called Cinderella story, so to speak, is over with," Dick Davey told the *Mercury News*.

The experts were right. With its athletic lineup and suffocating defence, Mississippi State was just too much for Santa Clara. The Broncos never led during the game, played in front of 11,853 fans, and eventually fell 75-67.

A running jumper by Steve pulled Santa Clara to within three, at 43-40, early in the second half. But that was as close as the Broncos would get as MSU guard T.J. Honore answered with a three-pointer to quell the rally.

Still, the game provided another showcase for Steve's growing talents. The Santa Clara junior kept the Broncos in the game, never allowing the Bulldogs' lead to get higher than ten points. In fact, three times during the final 20 minutes, the Broncos pulled to within a single shot of MSU.

Despite his sore ankle, Steve marked his second trip to the Big Dance with a 22-point performance on seven-for-13 shooting. His assist total was a mere two, but several of his pinpoint passes seemed a notch above what his teammates could handle. They were either bobbled inside or wasted by wide open shots that were off the mark.

The Broncos had done a decent job defending MSU's six-foot-11, 255-pound centre Erick Dampier, collapsing around the gigantic player and holding him to 13 points and nine rebounds. But they hadn't expected Honore, the MSU guard who averaged just 9.9 points during the regular season, to go four-for-five from three-point range.

"I think we could beat that team. I think that was evident to everybody," Steve told the *Mercury News* afterward.

"He fought his tail off," Davey added of Steve's performance. "We couldn't play Nash at every position."

Afterward, MSU forward Marcus Grant rated Steve Nash as the best player the Bulldogs had faced all season, including Arkansas all-American Corliss Williamson. "I have not seen a better point guard on the college level, other than Chris Jackson," Honore told the *Mercury News*.

It had been a great season for Steve, with only better things to look forward to as a senior since virtually the entire Santa Clara lineup was scheduled to return that fall.

"For some reason, it's not that tough right now," Steve told the *Mercury News* in the wake of the loss. "I have a feeling it'll hurt a lot more tomorrow and the next day."

The relationship between a basketball coach and his star player is seldom a simple one. Each counts on the other in crucial situations. Each disappoints the other from time to time. But both need each other more often than is probably conducive to producing an easy friendship. That's how the system works.

The relationship between Steve Nash and Dick Davey was perhaps typically rocky in the sense that they are both strong-minded individuals who hate to lose. And often their ideas about how to go about winning clashed. "They're still learning about how to deal with each other," observed graduated point guard John Woolery after a game during Steve's senior season. "There are obviously going to be conflicts. Both of them want to win."

Certainly, there was often fire between Dick Davey and Steve Nash. But something between them had also created a special magic at Santa Clara.

"Oh, we had some set-tos, yeah," Davey said, describing their relationship. "You know, he was a tough-minded competitor and fairly independent in his thinking at times. And you know, probably the biggest problem was that I never expected failure from him in any area. I expected perfection from Steve at a young age and that was my mistake.

"I told him when he started at Santa Clara, I said: 'You should lead the nation in free-throw shooting. You're that good a shooter. You should take care of the ball and rarely turn it over …' I had such high expectations for him. After a couple of games when he didn't perform at the level I thought he should be, I was discouraged with his performance a little bit. I let him know about

it and that I thought he could do better than he was. And I think it frustrated him a little bit."

Jason (Jake) Sedlock, Steve's four-year roommate at SCU and one of his best friends, saw the relationship between the coach and his star point guard in a unique light.

"In sophomore year, I was kind of skeptical that Steve might leave," Sedlock said. "He was really unhappy. And that was probably the time that I've seen him most unhappy and when I could really see it affect him."

"Coach Davey was on Steve all the time," Sedlock continued. "I think he could see the potential that Steve had and he was riding him hard to get it out. That's just his coaching style. I don't know if I would do that [as a coach]. Maybe I would. I can't say because I'm not in that position."

The tension between Steve Nash and Dick Davey reached its zenith during sophomore season. It would ease during his final two years at the school, as the two got more comfortable dealing with each other.

"We had one minor incident in Portland [in sophomore season] and it was completely my fault," Davey said before Nash's senior season began. "Steve missed a shot that I expected him to make and I thought maybe his decisions in that situation weren't good. I got on him and he came off the court and he was pissed. He's kind of an emotional player … Occasionally, I won't like something he does … I like players to keep their mouths shut and play. That's been a little bit of a transition for him. He's been headstrong and had his own way at times. But he's changed a little bit in that respect, got more mature."

During his career at Santa Clara, Steve Nash was one of the NCAA's top free-throw shooters.

"He was trying to grow and I expected him to be The Man right away," Davey continued, reflecting on the sophomore struggles. "I think I put added pressure on him to perform at a higher level and possibly expected too much, too soon. He had trouble dealing with that and I had trouble dealing with that because I always expected more from him and I still do today."

Through it all, the Santa Clara head coach always felt that Steve was tough enough to handle the added demands and the tests of character he was receiving. He believed being hard on Steve early would make him a tougher player in the long run.

"I wanted to see how he would handle pressure and different situations," Davey said. "He was tough-minded enough to hang in through it and, obviously, I think I was looking ahead that: 'If he can make it through this, we're going to have a great one. But if he's going to be in doubt as to whether or not he belongs here, then I'm never going to get out of him what I want to get out of him'."

"I think the thing that kept him involved with our program [early on] is he had a tremendous respect for his teammates," Davey added. "He really liked his teammates. If it had just been him and I at that time I think he probably would have said: 'See you later.' He would have got tired of my act."

There is no disputing, however, that Davey's "act" ultimately allowed Steve Nash to reach his goal. There is certainly no guarantee he would have been given the same kind of chance to shine by another coach or another program. And in fact, had Dick Davey for some reason failed to recognize Steve's potential on that fateful evening in the PNE Agrodome, he may not have played in the NCAA at all.

"In all fairness to him, he could have played at any program in the country," Davey said. "He may not have had the chance to become The Guy as soon at a bigger school, he might have had to sit. I'm not sure Steve would have liked that. At Santa Clara, he got the opportunity right away and the challenge right away, too."

Steve Nash has great respect for Dick Davey's competitiveness and his knowledge of the game. But he will probably never understand or agree with the reasoning behind some of the tactics used by the Broncos coach during his early years at Santa Clara. Although their relationship improved as Davey gave him more freedom and latitude during his junior and senior seasons, Steve describes most of his first two years in the program simply as "hell".

"Some of it, he was probably trying to get me better, trying to push me," Nash said. "Secondly, he was probably trying to test me mentally, see how tough I was. But there was the dimension that seemed like it went too far that makes me wonder why … It was sort of unreasonable. He was so extreme it's hard to say that he was really trying to make me a stronger person."

"But I'm glad I went through it. It's made me a tougher person and I thank him for that."

Dick Davey is thankful himself that the Canadian kid fell into his lap at Santa Clara and stayed there.

"I would love to have the opportunity to coach a lot of Steve Nashes in the next ten years," Davey said just before Steve's senior year tipped off. "He's so enjoyable to coach from the standpoint of the demands he puts on himself … He's made himself the player he is. I'd like to take a lot of credit. But, truthfully, I can't.

"I've had two players in all the years I've been involved in coaching who have been willing to go beyond the coach's demands. Kurt Rambis is one and Steve Nash is the other."

Chapter Six

THE CANADIAN NATIONAL TEAM

They sat in the bleachers at Lambrick Park high school, not more than 20 feet apart.

And although just a ninth-grader at the time, Steve Nash was keenly aware of the tall, thin, bespectacled man sitting near him. It was Ken Shields, the coach of the Canadian national men's basketball team.

It wasn't unusual to see Ken and his wife Kathy, the University of Victoria women's coach and an assistant with the women's national team, out watching a local high school tournament during the winter of 1988-89. Indeed, the Shields had long been a fixture in the gyms of Victoria, the capital city's version of roundball's royal couple.

Steve knew all about Ken Shields and his legendary record at UVic. He also knew that Ken Shields had absolutely no idea who he was. But as Steve sat there watching this high school tournament with some of his junior high buddies, he flirted with the idea of walking over to Shields, introducing himself and saying: "Hi. I'm going to play on the national team one day."

Steve Nash resisted the temptation this time. After all, he was only a junior high school kid. But he had a dream. And some day, he would figure into Ken Shields' plans. Of that he was sure.

That day arrived sooner than even Steve Nash, with his truckload full of self-confidence, could have imagined. Ken Shields carries a reputation in Canadian basketball circles as a stern taskmaster and, likely due to his sharp features as much as his intense personality, is known by many around Victoria simply as The Hawk. By the time Steve Nash had transferred from Mount Douglas to SMUS and was sitting out his grade 11 season, The Hawk had already decided to take this talented Victoria youngster under his wing.

In fact, by this time Shields had heard all about Nash, the junior high prodigy, from former UVic co-worker and national team player Howard Kelsey, who offered glowing reports on the teenager after "ratball" games in UVic's McKinnon Gym. And although he hadn't actually ever seen Steve play at Arbutus, Shields had visited one of the team's practices during Nash's grade ten year. The buzz had been out early on this wunderkind. It was clear he had some special skills.

After Steve had transferred to SMUS during that tumultuous grade 11 year, Shields started receiving rave reviews from Blue Devils coach Ian Hyde-Lay about his star point guard. Like his former coach at UVic, Hyde-Lay was not prone to exaggeration. Shields knew Steve Nash was legitimate.

With his national team scheduled to assemble for a ten-day try-out camp in Victoria in the spring of 1991, Shields made what, upon reflection, was a rather bold move. He invited Steve Nash, barely 17-years-old, to join in the national team workouts at McKinnon Gym.

Shields was well aware that a player this young had never been with the Senior Nats before. But he was also confident Steve could cope with the challenge. The confident manner in which this kid played, his skill level, quickness and understanding of the game would allow him to hold his own, Shields decided. And besides, this wasn't really a try-out. It was designed to give a potential future national-teamer some valuable experience.

"I never would have asked a kid his age to come in if I didn't think that he would cope well with it or that it was going to be good for him," Shields says now, reflecting on a move that obviously was a factor in Steve Nash's rapid development as a player. "If I'd thought that he wouldn't have been able to handle it or he might have been blown away or overwhelmed, I wouldn't have put him in there."

Steve Nash didn't disappoint Ken Shields during this camp, either. From the national team coach's perspective, the youngster performed solidly, looking after the ball and not appearing to be intimidated or in awe of anyone. Moreover, the other players seemed to respond to this kid and he interacted well with them. Although in terms of age, size and experience, he was in well over his head, it was also clear that Steve Nash was in his element.

"I remember he got picked once or twice, but it wasn't like he was out of place. Let me tell you, he was *not* out of place," Shields says now. "And here he was, a grade 11 player, playing with some guys who have played in the NBA."

Ken Shields had quickly taken a special interest in Steve Nash. This kid reminded him of another young point guard whom he had been fortunate enough to handle early on in his coaching career.

Shields' first men's head coaching job had come at Laurentian University in Sudbury. In that chilly, Ontario mining city, he had noticed a skinny junior high kid constantly hanging around his team's practices. This youngster had amazing skills and a feel for the game that extended well beyond his years.

That player was Eli Pasquale, who would go on to become one of the greatest guards in Canadian Interuniversity Athletic Union (CIAU) history and a 11-year backbone of Canada's national team program. But back in the early '70s, Eli was just a tough little Italian-Canadian teenager with a ball and a dream.

"Eli would hang around Laurentian and when we needed a player he'd be there to pop in," Shields recalls. "He'd fit in, too. We had very, very competitive scrimmages. Guys who lost had to sit out. Eli got to know that if he wanted to play, he had to look after the ball and he took great pride in trying to make his team win so they could stay on the floor, even though he was just a young kid."

Ken Shields left Laurentian in 1976, moving west to take the job as head men's basketball coach at UVic. And after graduating from Sudbury's Lockerby high school three years later, Eli Pasquale followed the coach out to Victoria. With Eli running his offence, Shields' Vikes rolled off five straight CIAU national titles, part of an incredible string of seven consecutive Canadian university championships that Shields would engineer on the UVic bench.

More than a decade later, as Shields watched Steve Nash develop, he couldn't help but draw comparisons to Eli Pasquale. He knew they had been much different kinds of kids; Pasquale a more disciplined and serious student of the game, Nash wilder and more creative.

The forerunner to Steve Nash, Eli Pasquale might well have succeeded in the NBA himself under different circumstances.

"Steve was wild as a player, very wild," Shields says now. "He did a lot of *stuff*. He was very good with the ball but a lot of the things he did didn't accomplish anything. He was always going behind his back and through his legs when he wasn't really using it to attack a defender or to improve his position, or as part of the game."

Eli Pasquale had not possessed the same kind of flamboyance or rebellious streak as Steve Nash. Nevertheless, Shields saw plenty of similarities between the two. The rock-solid confidence and the ability of both players to step in and compete at levels beyond their years were similar. So was the incredible amount of time each was willing to spend in the gym.

During the 1991 national team camp, Ken

Shields would have the rare opportunity to see both Eli Pasquale and Steve Nash on the same practice floor. The two entered the camp posting the highest fitness test scores in national team history. They would practise against one another for ten days that spring — the present and the future of the Canadian backcourt. For Shields and avid followers of the national team, it was a delicious prelude to the changing of the guard.

Steve Nash was a little intimidated by his first national team experience. Here he was, barely 17, playing with basketball names he had grown up hearing about. Sure, many of these guys hadn't played in the NCAA, but Steve didn't need any prompting to recognize UVic greats Eli Pasquale and Gerald Kazanowski or Mike Smrek, an Ontario seven-footer with a couple of NBA championship rings from his days with the Los Angeles Lakers in the late '80s.

Steve, who was far younger, was also much smaller physically than these players. In one sense, he lacked confidence on the court during those ten days at McKinnon Gym. In another, the experience buoyed his confidence. He had already attained one of his major goals, and at such a young age. He was up against Canada's best basketball players and he definitely wasn't getting blown away.

Nevertheless, at the same time, Steve often felt outplayed, like he was somehow underachieving. At 17, he was already accustomed to dominating every sports scenario and this was a foreign sensation.

Steve would use this experience to learn every day, on the floor and off. One afternoon after a practice, Leo Rautins, a first-round NBA draft choice by the Philadelphia 76ers in 1983, stopped the high schooler in a UVic hallway. Rautins, who had come out of Toronto private school St. Michaels to join the national team as a teenager himself, told Steve about some of his experiences playing college basketball at Syracuse. He believed Steve had the potential to play in the NCAA, too.

"You need to start shooting the ball more," Rautins told him. "You can already pass and penetrate and handle the ball, but a point guard who can shoot and do all those other things is *really* important to a team."

The following December, in the midst of Steve's grade 12 season at SMUS, Ken Shields planned a special trip to a SuperSonics-Golden State Warriors game in Seattle. Accompanying him on the journey from Victoria were Steve Nash and his high school coach, Ian Hyde-Lay.

Shields didn't tell Steve the purpose behind the trip. But he wanted the Victoria youngster to get a close-up look at point guard Tim Hardaway of the Golden State Warriors. At the time, Steve wasn't weight-training and the national team coach wanted to encourage him to get stronger.

Shields arranged the trip through the Warriors, a team he had been an observer with in training camp that fall. The seats provided by assistant coach Donn Nelson were great, right behind the Warriors' bench in the Seattle coliseum. The Golden State players were wearing long-sleeved outfits as they warmed up. And just as the Warriors peeled off their warm-ups before the tip-off, Shields nudged Steve.

"Check out Hardaway," Shields nodded.

The Warriors point guard took off his jacket and Steve's eyes bugged out as he let out a slight gasp: "Oh my God!" he said as he observed Hardaway's upper-body. The guy was built like a tank.

"If you want to play in the NBA," Shields said, "that's the kind of body you've got to have."

Steve was a big fan of Hardaway, a smallish point guard who had nevertheless succeeded in the NBA and become famous for his lightning-quick cross-over dribble. After the game, Shields introduced Steve to Nelson, the Golden State assistant who had agreed to introduce the high schooler to Tim Hardaway.

Hardaway and Nash walked together from the locker room to the Golden State bus. The Warriors star had a few brief words of advice.

"I just told him pushups," Hardaway recalls now. "That's what I do, pushups, and I do a lot of weights for my lower body."

Probably more important than any technical advice he received that day was the fact that Steve Nash had been given an opportunity to talk with an NBA player whom he admired. The experience brought him one step closer to his dream.

Shields believed the trip and the chance to see Tim Hardaway would be valuable for Steve. Physical strength was the one quality Shields felt Eli Pasquale had lacked in his attempt to make the NBA. After being drafted by Seattle in the fifth round of the 1984 draft, 106th overall, Pasquale had been one of the final cuts from Sonics' camp.

The following October, Eli was again among the last cuts after playing through the exhibition season with the Chicago Bulls often as the backcourt partner of Michael Jordan.

In the years following, Shields had come to the conclusion that Pasquale's body wasn't "NBA strong". He was determined to help Steve Nash gain that edge for when his time came.

"I encouraged Steve to get strong," Shields says now. "And he has. His body has significantly developed."

By the summer of '93, between his freshman and sophomore years at Santa Clara, Steve Nash had moved from the periphery of the national-team program to the forefront. Eli Pasquale had retired from the Senior Nats after breaking an ankle just days before the 1992 Olympic qualifying tournament began in Portland. The Nats needed a new floor general and this was the summer he was scheduled to arrive.

Steve started out on Canada's under-22 national team for the second straight summer as it attempted to qualify for the following year's world championships. The team ended up narrowly failing to qualify but the experience of playing in the Americas tournament, under the "interesting" conditions that Argentina can offer, would prove invaluable for this group of emerging Canadian players.

During the qualifying tournament, some 9,000 fans packed a stadium for Canada's game against host Argentina, the eventual champions. True to form for passionate South American crowds,

spectators threw candy, ice and coins onto the floor during the game. Steve was hit in the back of the neck by an iceball the size of a baseball. After that loss to Argentina, which had included a brawl between players from the two countries, the Canadian contingent needed an armed police escort to escape the hostile crowd. It had been an eye-opening welcome to international basketball.

Perhaps Steve Nash's greatest moment to date in a national team uniform came about a month later during the 1993 World University Games in Buffalo. Heading into the Games, not a lot was expected of the Canadians, particularly in light of their failure to qualify down in Argentina. But, led by Steve Nash, the Student Nats would turn in a memorable performance in Buffalo.

The American squad for the Student Games had been dubbed the Mini Dream Team and it featured an all-star cast of young NCAA talent, including Damon Stoudamire, Michael Finley, Carlos Rogers, Ed O'Bannon and Shawn Respert. None of the other

Wearing Canada across his chest in international play has been both a thrill and an important developmental tool for Steve Nash.

countries were given any kind of chance against the Americans, particularly since the Games were being played on U.S. soil. Certainly the Canadian squad, whose "name" players were Steve Nash, Jeff Foreman of Winnipeg, Brandon's Keith Vassell, Sean Van Koughnett of Waterloo and Toronto's Rowan Barrett, weren't considered any kind of a threat to the U.S. gold medal march.

But during the lead-up portion to the University Games, the Canadians performed surprisingly well against the U.S. The teams split a pair of loosely-organized exhibition scrimmages at Toronto's Humber College, with Steve more than holding his own against both Stoudamire and Kentucky's Travis Ford. "They're a more talented team on paper," Steve told *Sports Ink* newspaper after those games. "But when you take that away, it's just two basketball teams. I'm really looking forward to going for a medal this week — and not just a silver or a bronze."

Being part of a major Games for the first time was a huge thrill for Steve. He liked the atmosphere in the Games village, where all the athletes lived and socialized together. He roomed with fellow Victorian and future Santa Clara teammate Brendan Graves in Buffalo and it was so hot they had to leave their door and windows wide open. At night, everyone on the Canadian team would hang out together because only one room in the village had a fan. It was a colourful, friendly atmosphere and the Canadian players grew close.

Canada continued to perform well on the court in Buffalo, too, crushing Japan by a 99-53 margin and then running down Sweden 86-68 behind Steve's steady 17-point effort. In its quarter-final pool, Canada downed China 84-75 before clinching a semi-final berth with an 82-76 decision over the Czech Republic, a game in which Steve hit some crucial free-throws down the stretch to stem a Czech comeback.

With an average age of just over 20, Canada had one of the youngest lineups in the 16-team Student Games field. Nevertheless, the Canadians outlasted a more experienced Italian lineup 77-74 in their semi-final and seemed to be rounding into form at precisely the right time as they prepared to meet the powerful U.S. in the gold-medal game.

The Canadians, though obviously surprised and delighted to be in the final, were also a little taken aback by the attitude surrounding the U.S. team. One U.S. newspaper had written, essentially, that the championship game would simply be the seventh day of a seven-day basketball clinic for the rest of the world. The media was forecasting a blowout of major proportions and they weren't getting too many arguments.

But when the gold-medal game tipped off in a nearly sold-out Memorial Auditorium, the Canadians were ready. Led by Steve Nash, Canada ran out to an unbelievable 17-point lead early in the contest and they managed to enter the dressing room at half-time holding onto a 12-point advantage. The Americans seemed to be in shock as they headed dejectedly for their locker room. Each of these U.S. players was a major college star in his own right and Steve could sense they were all nervous. Meanwhile, the crowd at the Aud seemed to be in shock as well.

In the second half, the more talented Americans clawed back, putting together a 16-0 run and taking their first lead with 15 minutes to play. Damon Stoudamire, all too familiar with Steve Nash after Santa Clara's huge upset over Arizona that same spring in the NCAA Tournament, did not want to perish at the hands of a Canadian again. Stoudamire scored a clutch basket to put the U.S. ahead by five, at 93-88, with just over a minute to play. The Canadians didn't let up, but the U.S. managed to hang on for a white-knuckle 95-90 decision over a team which logic dictated they should have beaten easily.

U.S. head coach Reggie Minton of Air Force and his assistants Bob Huggins of Cincinnati and Jim Harrick of UCLA breathed a huge sigh of relief. They had managed to avoid the fate of the 1983 U.S. team, a glittering array of stars led by Charles Barkley and Karl Malone, that had been upset by Canada in the Edmonton World University Games.

"Goliath won but, boy, did he have to work," Doug Smith of the Canadian Press wrote in several newspapers across the country the next day.

The Americans had avoided an embarrassing upset, but just barely. And if there had been any doubts after Santa Clara's spring run that Steve Nash was the real deal, there were certainly none now. Winnipeg's Jeff Foreman led Canada with 30 points and nine rebounds, but Nash had steered the Canadians through the pressure of the gold-medal game, scoring 11 points and dishing out a staggering 17 assists.

"It was a great game," Steve would say afterward. "That's the kind of atmosphere you like to play in. We had them. We should have beat them."

Just how close this U.S. team had come to losing on home soil had not escaped the media. Larry Felser, sports editor of the Buffalo News, penned a post-game column under the headline: "Canadians can walk away with heads held high."

"Imagine a gold medal in basketball at stake and the U.S. nearly got impaled on it ..." Felser wrote. "This was supposed to be one of America's famous basketball barbecues, by invitation only. It turned out that the Americans had to fight just to keep off the grill themselves."

"I was proudest of the fact that, playing a team as good as the U.S., with all the pressure they put on us, on their home court, in front of their fans, our kids did not give in to their nerves," Canadian coach Dave Nutbrown told the News. "There are pros playing for big money who can't do that."

The Student Games would be just one part of a hectic summer of '93 for Steve Nash. After Buffalo, he would go on to represent B.C. in the Canada Games at Kamloops. And from there, it was on to the senior national team for the world championship qualifying tournament in Puerto Rico.

Actually, after a mixed-age national team camp in Toronto at the beginning of that same summer, Ken Shields had been ready to keep Steve with the Senior Nats for the duration. But the world under-22 qualification tournament team had needed the skills of the slick 19-year-old point guard and Shields reasoned that the University Games in Buffalo would be a good experience for Nash as well. He felt it was important for Steve to get a chance to run his own team and establish himself in a leadership role.

By the end of the summer, however, Steve had logged considerably more court time and air miles than any other member of the national team program. It was obvious that he was being groomed to run Shields' offence the following summer in Toronto, when Canada would play host to the world.

It was about this time that the fatigue factor was brought up when people mentioned Steve's name. There was speculation that all this national-team work, as well as a rigorous college basketball routine, would have Steve burned out before his sophomore year at Santa Clara was over.

"The best players in the NBA — to get to the NBA — log day after day after day, hour upon hour in the gym," Shields says. "So, all this crap about burn-out is a trendy thing. I told Steve: 'Don't let anybody tell you you're going to get burned out with the national team. You want to play and, if you weren't playing for us, you'd be in the gym at home'."

As the summer of '94 approached, Steve Nash eagerly looked forward to a chance no Canadian basketball player had ever had before. He and the rest of his Senior Nats teammates would be going after a major world championship in their own country.

The 1994 World Championship of Basketball was the first major senior international hoops competition that Canada had staged since the 1976 Montreal Olympics. The tournament would include the luminaries of Dream Team II and a smattering of other NBA players suiting up for their respective countries. This was a tremendous chance to raise basketball's profile in the Canadian consciousness, especially with the dawn of NBA expansion franchises in Toronto and Vancouver only a year away.

But being the host country would not turn out to be much of an advantage for Canada. In a pre-tournament article in the Toronto *Sun* entitled Unknown Soldiers, basketball writer Craig Daniels pointed out just how low-profile, in a national sense, Canada's best basketball players actually were.

"Just ask yourself if you would recognize Joey Vickery, Dwight Walton or Steve Nash if you bumped into them," Daniels wrote.

The world championship field included 16 countries and would be played in Toronto's Maple Leaf Gardens and SkyDome and Hamilton's Copps Coliseum over an 11-day period. Canada entered the competition never having finished better than sixth and was coming off a 12th-place showing at the previous Worlds in 1990 at Buenos Aires.

A pre-tournament promotional postcard, with players and coaches posed at the CN Tower read: "On Top of the World." It seemed rather optimistic, given the scenario Canada was facing as it prepared to open the tournament August 4 against Angola in the Gardens.

"The near shameful reality is that the Gardens' house that night, expected to be two-thirds full at best, will know virtually as much about Angola, Canada's opponent, as it will about its own team," Daniels wrote in his *Sun* article.

Ever the floor general, Steve Nash takes charge, whether in NCAA play, or on the international hardwood.

"The reality is that people in Brazil and Argentina are more familiar with what Canada has done than are Canadians," added the now-retired National team player Leo Rautins, a commentator for CTV during the Worlds.

Nevertheless, as the Canadians rode a strong pre-tournament exhibition performance into the world championships, everybody connected with the team felt this was a chance to improve the foothold of their sport in their own country. "There is a window of opportunity to have basketball impacted in a tremendously positive way," Ken Shields told the Toronto *Star*. "It may or may not happen. Whether we take full advantage of it remains to be seen."

"Around the world, a lot of people don't have respect for our team and that's good," Steve told Canadian Press before the tournament. "It excites us because we want to get out on the floor and show people they should respect us."

Several outside factors had gone against the Nats heading into this tournament, however. Basketball Canada had slashed $250,000 from its national teams' budget just months before the tournament, leaving Shields in the unenviable position of having to solicit donations and sponsorships to keep his program running at a time when he should have been able to devote all his energies to coaching and preparation.

Another problem was brewing in the Canadian backcourt. Nash had come along nicely, scoring 28 points and adding 11 assists in a win over Spain during the European tour, his coming-out performance as a senior international player. Shields had already long since decided that Nash was going to be his starting point guard rather than the incumbent Ronn McMahon. After making a couple of trips to Santa Clara to monitor Steve's progress during the winter, he knew that Nash was improving every day. "He's definitely our best point guard already," Shields thought.

"He's young but he doesn't play young," Shields told Canadian Press just before the world tournament started. "He's very composed on the basketball court so he's capable of starting for us. I've seen him play since junior high, so I know what his talent is."

Shields' decision didn't sit well with McMahon, an intense five-foot-nine fireplug of a player who had become the Senior Nats' starting point guard in the two years since Eli Pasquale retired. McMahon didn't appreciate what he considered to be a demotion. When Shields told him of his decision, McMahon said he would accept it, but he seemed to do so reluctantly.

Steve would go on to start the entire world tournament as a 20-year-old, getting about 70 per cent of the minutes at point guard. McMahon had to make do with coming off the bench and he wasn't thrilled about it. But while McMahon's reaction created some uneasiness on the team, most of the other Nats seemed to accept that their young oncourt quarterback deserved to be where he was.

"It didn't help Steve and it didn't help Ronn. It certainly didn't help the team," Shields says now. "I don't know whether Ronn felt it was owed to him by seniority, but that's not the way things work. The best guy that can be on the floor has to be there and, in that case, it happened to be Steve."

The 1994 edition of the Nats was an odd collection of Westerners (J.D. Jackson, Greg Wiltjer, Spencer McKay, Joey Vickery, McMahon and Nash), Easterners (Mike Smrek, Martin Keane, Kory Hallas, Will Njoku and Dwight Walton) and just one NBA regular — Boston Celtics swingman Rick Fox.

Canada headed into the Worlds with an 8-1 record in pre-tournament international play. But it also headed into a field that included some of the best basketball talent on the planet. Croatia boasted NBAers Toni Kukoc and Dino Radja. And the U.S. Dream Team II featured Derrick Coleman, Joe Dumars, Kevin Johnson, Larry Johnson, Shawn Kemp, Dan Majerle, Reggie Miller, Alonzo Mourning, Shaquille O'Neal, Mark Price, Steve Smith and Dominique Wilkins.

Unlike their predecessors in 1992, however, this edition of the Canadian team would not have the chance to experience a Dream matchup.

Ken Shields' '92 squad had met Dream Team I — with Magic Johnson, Larry Bird, Michael Jordan, et al — during the Olympic qualifying tournament in Portland. But the draw didn't work out that way for the '94 Nats in Toronto. This time, Canada was seeded into a four-team preliminary round-robin pool with Russia, Angola and Argentina. The top two teams from each of the four pools would advance to one of two playoff round-robin pools. The best two teams from each playoff pool would then go on to the medal round.

"I don't think many people in Toronto know who we are or even what we are, but I think we've got a good chance." Steve told the Toronto *Star* in a pre-tournament story.

Steve would start Canada's first game at Maple Leaf Gardens, against Angola, despite an injury to the arch of his right foot that had occurred in

Europe and kept him out of serious workouts for ten days.

His first major international start for the senior Nats was a solid one, nonetheless. The 20-year-old point guard scored seven of Canada's first 13 points before picking up two quick fouls and heading for the bench for a good portion of the game.

Canada would cruise to an easy 83-52 victory over Angola in the game in front of about 8,000 fans at the Gardens. But compared to earlier tournament games that day featuring Greece and Croatia, the historic Toronto arena was practically devoid of emotion for Canada's debut.

Canada built on its first win by beating Argentina 91-73 in its second game in front of a much livelier crowd of about 9,000 in the Gardens. The victory assured Canada of at least eighth place in the tournament and a coveted spot in the quarter-final round.

Canada's third game had a pumped-up Copps Coliseum crowd of 11,000 in Hamilton on its feet the whole way. But the Nats would eventually fall 73-66 to Russia, giving in to a 12-2 Russian run during the final three-and-a-half minutes. Still, the loss actually served Canada well, because it meant the host country would not be placed in the same playoff pool as the powerful U.S.

Canada instead advanced to a quarter-final pool along with Greece, Croatia and China. With the China game considered an easy win and powerful Croatia rated as the second-best team in the tournament behind the U.S., it appeared that Canada's chances of advancing into medal play hinged on the showdown with Greece.

Greece and Canada were tabbed to meet in the first game of the quarter-final round. A win would most likely move Canada into the medal round; a loss meant no realistic shot at getting there. It was a pressure situation and, to make things worse for Canada, it appeared the Nats' home-court advantage would be nothing of the sort.

Canada had already spent much of the tournament feeling like visitors in its own country, what with the Dream Team II getting most of the ink and Toronto's ethnic communities throwing feverish support behind some of the other visiting nations. For the Canadian players, some of whom had gone as far as to have maple leafs tattooed on their chests and most of whom had dedicated the better part of a year preparing for this tournament, it hurt.

"We've got to get a Canadian crowd in here," Shields told the Canadian Press on the eve of his team's biggest game of the tournament.

"The people should support us," added forward Kory Hallas. "We're representing Canada at a tournament in Canada and we should have the fans behind us."

It wouldn't turn out that way, however. In the Monday night Gardens crowd of 11,088 for this important Canada-Greece showdown, the majority of the fans seemed to be waving the light blue and white flag of Greece. Canadian players were even greeted with scattered boos as they took their "homecourt" before the game.

"It's pretty hard for a Canadian kid to play in his own country and get booed," Shields would say later. "That shouldn't happen."

Whether lack of support had anything to do with the outcome of this pivotal game is debatable. But Canada's tournament fortunes certainly hinged on the outcome against Greece. The game boiled down to one, tension-filled play.

A pair of three-pointers by Kory Hallas had cut a seven-point Greek lead to just a single point with 1:19 to play. Then, with the ball and a chance for the win with 24 seconds left, Canada took a time-out. In the ensuing huddle, Shields agreed to let Rick Fox, his lone NBA veteran, take the ball one-on-one on the penultimate play. Fox would try to score, draw a foul or create something for a teammate.

But with the game clock down to just seven seconds and Canada's fate hanging agonizingly in the balance, Fox stumbled while trying to spin-dribble in the key. The basketball slipped out of his hands. Greece recovered and whipped the ball quickly downcourt to Panagiotis Fassoulas, who sealed matters with a slam dunk to give his country a 74-71 win.

Technically, Canada's medal hopes were still alive. Realistically, they were toast. Canada now needed a victory over powerful Croatia in order to move on and they wouldn't even come close, falling 92-61 two days later to NBAers Dino Radja (25 points), Toni Kukoc (15 points) and their talented teammates. It was during this painful loss that the finger-pointing and bitterness on the Canadian bench began to surface as some players' composure dissolved under the unbearable weight of disappointment.

Canada would go on to place seventh in the world tournament, its best finish since 1982. But an 85-82 loss to Puerto Rico spoiled the host country's chances of placing fifth. For Canada, the world tournament ended quietly, with a 104-76 victory over China in a morning consolation game in front of only 1,000 fans at Copps Coliseum. Canada's players, who had trained so long for this, had expected more.

"When you lose close games, you tend to lose a bit of perspective," Ken Shields told the Canadian Press. "We have a lot to be proud of."

That's not the way many in the Eastern sports media saw things, however. Shields was drawing heavy fire in Toronto over what was being portrayed in some quarters as an embarrassing world championship performance. He was being painted as a coach far too preoccupied with the technical aspects of the game, a coach who refused to let his athletes "play". This was ironic considering the fact the Nats had run a motion offence during the world tournament, giving the Canadian players a great deal of opportunity to create on the court.

Shields was being heavily criticized for his alleged lack of personality and poor communication skills. He had become the convenient scapegoat for what was perceived by some as a major underachievement by the host Canadian team. "There are guys who were just waiting for the opportunity to take their shots," Shields told Canadian Press as the tournament concluded.

"No one wants to win more than Ken," one anonymous player told the Canadian Press. "We still respect the guy and appreciate what he's done for us … He did everything he believed was the best for the team. Sometimes it's implied that he didn't do what was best and that's what hurts. To take one person out and really dig into him, we don't think that's right."

Utah coach Rick Majerus, a Dream Team II assistant, probably put the whole controversy in perspective best when he told Canadian Press: "If [Rick] Fox makes that basket [against Greece], all's right in the world and Ken's the saviour of basketball in Canada. When I see some of the criticism of Ken in that regard, it's obviously not coming from basketball people."

Shields would resign from his national team post four months after the world tournament, a move he had been planning for awhile. But before he quit, he felt he had to address allegations made against his program by Wayne Yearwood and Cordell Llewellyn, players who had left the team before the Worlds. The two players, who had been released for disciplinary reasons, happened to be black. Shields' roster move had resulted in thinly-veiled hints from some corners in Eastern Canada that racism influenced national-team personnel decisions. The controversy was further fuelled by a post-tournament freelance article in the Toronto *Globe and Mail* that was based on the allegations of the two players.

Shields didn't want to leave the national team job under the cloud that this controversy had created. He demanded that an independent review be established to look into the released players' allegations. A three-person panel subsequently interviewed 65 people and didn't find a single shred of evidence of racism in the national team program.

Shields doesn't believe the controversy had any measurable affect on his team's chemistry at the worlds. But it couldn't have come at a worse time.

"It might have affected some of the black guys on the team because they were under a lot of pressure from the black community," Shields says now. "There were undercurrents in the community that Yearwood and Llewellyn got the shaft."

Steve Nash remembers the situation being discussed by national team players and he doesn't believe it was particularly good for the team to be focusing on this kind of an issue with such a big test looming in Toronto. But he also believes the only problem between Shields and the cut players was one of communication.

"Ken's not racist," Steve says. "He never was and he never will be. He might have had a problem relating sometimes to some black players. But it wasn't the colour of their skin, it was the person he had trouble with."

The *Globe and Mail* eventually ran an apology and agreed to an undisclosed financial settlement with Shields. But that controversy, along with the stinging criticism Shields had taken in the media after the world tournament, left a sour taste in his mouth.

These things disheartened Shields but they weren't what prompted him to resign a national-team coaching job that he had always dreamed of holding. In fact, Shields had decided to quit a full four months prior to the world tournament when his national teams' budget had been slashed a whopping $250,000 by Basketball Canada.

"It was the best thing I ever did, to get away from there," Shields says now.

When a position as head of the new Commonwealth Centre for Sport Development opened up, Ken Shields jumped at it. And basketball in Canada lost one of its finest people.

By the summer of 1995, people were talking about the new direction of Canada's national team. But to veteran observers of the Nats, things looked pretty familiar.

Ken Shields was gone and Steve Konchalski, a Maritimer, had taken his place. But as usual, Canada was looking at throwing together a team in short order in an attempt to qualify for the Atlanta Olympics.

This time, Canada would have to do without any NBA help as both Rick Fox and Bill Wennington were unavailable. And this time, that qualifying road would wind its way through Argentina.

Canada would need to survive a ten-game, 13-day ordeal in South America if it hoped to be one of three teams from the Americas zone to emerge with an Olympic berth for the following summer.

Tales of South American conditions have become legendary among national team members. Eli Pasquale tells of games where coins were launched from the stands at visiting players. Greg Wiltjer, a Sidney, B.C. native and veteran of the national team program, remembers lighters and keys being tossed. He also recalls a game in Peru in which the teams had to actually play in a cage to protect players and officials from the fans.

The Canadians opened the tournament at Tucuman, where the basketball stadium had only three walls completed. A gigantic tarp stood in place of much of the fourth wall, stretching from the top of the bleachers to the roof and keeping out most of the elements. But some birds found their way into the facility, along with moisture and chilly breezes. The gym floor was cold and slippery. "It was just awful," Steve recalls.

Canada got off to a cold start, too, falling 82-79 to the Dominican Republic in its opener. Helped by Steve Nash's 12-point effort, the Nats battled back from 22 down early in the second half but couldn't complete the comeback. Things went from bad to worse in the second game, which Canada dropped 84-73 to Puerto Rico.

But the Canadian team then began a remarkable turnaround, winning five straight games as the tournament switched sites to Neuquen. Steve had 18 points in a 90-79 decision over Cuba and added 14 more in an important second-round 94-73 win over Uruguay. In perhaps Canada's biggest win of the tournament, Steve scored 13 points and nailed a pair of free throws during the final two minutes as Canada upset Brazil 104-99 to guarantee itself a semifinal spot and move just one win away from clinching a berth in Atlanta.

Unfortunately, that one win is always the toughest to nail down at these qualifying tournaments. Under Ken Shields, Canada had discovered that fact rather painfully when it fell by four points to Venezuela in Portland and narrowly missed out on a berth in the 1992 Barcelona Olympics.

"I like our chances to qualify. It'll be tough but I definitely think we can do it," Steve Nash said as he and his Canadian teammates headed into crunch time. "We're a young team with a whole new system and style of play. We're just coming together. I thought we would be a team that got better every game and that's what's happened."

"We have a lot of talent on this team," Steve added, "but a big key will be how we handle things mentally. It'll be interesting to see how we respond to that type of pressure."

Canada saw its first shot at an Olympic berth go out the window with a 98-81 loss to Puerto Rico, a game in which Steve had 12 points but was forced to the bench early with foul trouble. That loss, in which the Canadians never really contended, set the stage for a third-place showdown against Brazil. The winners would go to Atlanta in '96. The losers would stay home.

"If somebody at the beginning of the summer had said we'd have one game to get to the Olympics, I would have taken it in a minute," Steve Konchalski told Canadian Press. "Now we've got it and we have to take advantage of it. I have to pick these guys up and get them to play with a little emotion."

Canada had beaten Brazil in the second round of the tournament, but it couldn't repeat that performance in the clutch, falling 97-77 to the Brazilians and watching its Olympic dreams go down in flames. It was not a strong performance for the Nats, who made just ten of 19 free throws and shot just seven-for-25 from three-point range.

"The team that played the last two games certainly wasn't the team that won five in a row last week," Canadian coach Steve Konchalski told the Canadian Press. "What happened?"

Steve Nash believes several factors led to Canada's sudden collapse with an Olympic berth in sight. The team's chemistry was poor and it had been a tough grind living in Argentina for almost a month. "It was like a different planet," he says now, "totally different food, different conditions, different language ..."

"You know, if I sit here and think about it for a couple of minutes, I'll get ticked off. I'll get sad," he says. "I should have been playing in the Olympics. We definitely had the means to do it and we didn't get it done. It's really disappointing, especially because it's never going to be in Atlanta again."

Disappointment aside, Steve doesn't find it strange that Canada continues to struggle in major international basketball competition. The lack of a domestic professional league in Canada is a huge disadvantage for the Nats since Canadian players are usually scrambling to find pro contracts elsewhere. And when the national team plays at a major event, some players use that opportunity as an individual showcase. There is often competition among teammates for things such as court time and shots.

"The guys in the other countries are all playing professionally, getting paid a lot of money and they have a lot of security, stability and confidence," Nash explains. "Whereas, Canadian guys — they're not getting paid a lot of the time. They know they're just as good as the guy on Argentina, or another country, but they're not getting paid like that guy. So there's insecurity, because they want to show everyone that they should be getting paid and they want to use Canada as a stepping stone to a contract somewhere.

"So there's always that insecurity and defensiveness about Canadian players," he adds. "And you can't blame them. I mean, I'd probably feel the same way if I'm in their footsteps one day. It's tough when you're in that situation. It's your livelihood. So, a lot of times Canadian teams have hidden agendas because players are uncertain what they're going to be doing after the summer's over. Most guys on Canadian teams, the whole time these tournaments are going on, they're talking to agents: 'Can I get a job here? Can I get a job there?' And it's tough. I mean, how do you expect to deal with your livelihood and play on a team and not worry about a game as an audition? It's tough for guys and it hurts the team at times. But it's hard to really blame someone."

Ken Shields says that if he were still coaching, he wouldn't want to take players who weren't under contract to any major international event.

"It was the same thing at the Worlds," Shields says. "It was unbelievable. That was the single most divisive factor on our team — guys trying to get contracts. A couple of them, it absolutely destroyed their games. It was just ridiculous … Then they blame you for standing in their way of a contract. And their whole obsession is with a contract and not with performing for the team."

Making the NBA is the biggest thrill so far in Steve Nash's basketball life. But wearing the maple leaf and the word CANADA across his chest is probably a strong second.

Steve got the chance to wear the maple leaf earlier than most, appearing in his first senior national team scrimmage as a 17-year-old and sounding like a grizzled international veteran by age 22. He credits the time he has spent in the national team program as a major factor in his development into an NBA player. It has also been a dream come true.

"It's a big thrill. But I probably take it for granted in some ways because I've been doing it since I was 16- or 17- years-old," Steve says. "You probably lose sight of what it really means, at times. But at other times you really feel good about it. You go to another country and you're wearing that name across your chest and you feel like you really are representing the whole country. It's something you don't fully realize unless you sit down and think about it.

"I'm definitely 100 per cent proud of being Canadian," he adds. "I love Canada. My teammates at Santa Clara were probably sick of hearing about it. And definitely, I want kids from Canada and Victoria to see that they can compete and that they should be able to have the same goals and dreams that I had and that there's no reason they can't do the thing I'm doing.

"But once I get out there on the floor, you know, I just want to compete, Canadian or not … I just want to play."

That, in essence, is Steve Nash's philosophy. Being Canadian is something to be proud of. And in no way should it be any kind of liability for a basketball player as long as he or she is willing to work hard.

When he arrived at Santa Clara, many people wanted to stereotype Steve as a typical Canadian. Even after his junior year, *College Sports* magazine had him pose for a photo accompanying its major feature wearing a hockey-style jersey and holding a hockey stick, while stickhandling a basketball in the San Jose Arena. It was pretty goofy, but Steve realizes it was also the obvious story line. And that will likely continue to be the case for many years to come.

"People at Santa Clara always wanted to listen to see if I said: 'eh'," he laughs. "I never really said it, not even in high school. So I think people were sort of disappointed. But I think that was great because that way people kind of realized: 'Hey, if he doesn't say it, maybe that *is* a stereotype'."

Despite the fact he is now a professional, Steve Nash would still one day like to wear Canada's colours into the Olympics.

"Definitely, I want to go," he says without hesitation. "I really wanted to play in Atlanta. But it's not really the place that's important. It's just the setting. Going to the World University Games, being in the athletes' village there, really gave me a taste of it. A lot of people, superstar athletes, living in commons — it's really a great atmosphere. Being a part of the opening ceremony and all that was a lot of fun."

Ken Shields can't remember when Steve Nash first told him that he was going to play in the NBA. But it was well before the precocious teenager had become a fixture on his national team.

"He said it seriously and he didn't say it in a macho sense," Shields recalls. "I thought, hey: 'Maybe you can.'

"I was proud of him because he said it without bragging and he was going out on a limb, saying: 'I think I can do this.' He wasn't being a hero when he said it. He just pointedly said it. And you could tell when he said it, he had his mind set on it."

Ken Shields decided to help put some substance behind that dream. Throughout his career at UVic, Shields had always been a staunch believer that Canada should try to keep its best basketball players at Canadian schools. But when Steve Nash decided he wanted to go to the U.S., Shields helped him.

"I think it was good for him. I think in his case, it was the right decision," Shields says now.

"The only negative thing I see with Steve doing well at Santa Clara is that the exodus of Canadian talent in basketball just grows, and it does nothing for our sport in our country. You look at the CIAU championships the last three or four years and there's not one player who's going to be on the national team. All our best guys are gone. In the '80s, every one of our top UVic guys made the national team. Our guys were the starters on the national team. We took great pride in our kids going to national team try-out camp and kicking those guys' butts who were in NCAA schools.

"The best kids are going now. Our programs aren't keeping pace. Our institutions are downsizing athletics, right across the country. There is just not the emphasis, or leadership, or direction, or push to keep the good kids here. The good kids now don't even consider staying in Canada if there's any opportunity, *any* opportunity, to go to the States, and it's sad.

"And Steve going down there and getting all the ink that he did just makes it worse. Because more kids read it, and more kids think: 'I want to do that, I want to follow in Steve Nash's footsteps.' But that's not Steve's fault. That's our fault in the Canadian system for not making it more attractive and providing an equal opportunity, and an equal alternative."

Eli Pasquale, the outstanding Canadian point

guard of the '80s, didn't have the same opportunity to head south that Steve Nash had. But he doesn't begrudge the player who followed in his hightops, either.

"You've got to go for what you can get," Eli said shortly after Steve headed south. "Personally, I think that maybe I just didn't set my sights high enough when I was younger. I think when we won the gold medal [at the 1983 Edmonton World University Games], then I started to see it. But I think then that it was too late."

Certainly, Steve Nash had opportunities that some of his Canadian predecessors didn't. But something else also separates Steve from the thousands of other Canadian kids who dream of the NBA while shooting hoops in the driveway.

"I think a lot of it with Steve is attitude, desire to improve, love of the game, willingness to head for the gym when his buddies are going for a beer, single-mindedness, not being led astray by other people," Shields says. "Plus he has an innate capacity for the game. I mean, he understands. He has a natural intuition or feel for the game of basketball. And he probably has the same feel in soccer or the same feel in a lot of sports. And it's rare. The other thing Steve has is that rock-solid self-confidence."

Ken Shields and Steve Nash are similar in one key area. Both agree that Nash has beaten the odds against a Canadian making the NBA. But both fiercely believe that there is no inherent reason a Canadian can't compete just as hard as an American, a Greek, a Croat or a Brazilian on the basketball court.

"The odds against Steve making the NBA were huge," Shields says. "I mean, there's never been a

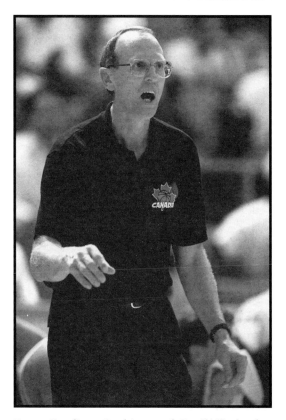

Former Canadian national team coach Ken Shields played an important role in Steve Nash's development into an NBA player.

player his size do what he's done in Canada. But he's earned it. He's put in his time. He has the right skill set, physically, mentally, socially, psychologically. He's got the whole package."

Perhaps most important of all, says Shields, is "the Canadian mentality hasn't beaten him down."

"It's hard to tell people when you're young that you'd like to play in the NBA and be taken seriously, especially in Canada," Steve says. "But it's always been a dream for me. I think the NBA is pretty much a dream for most kids who play basketball. And I think it's important not to let go of those dreams."

Chapter Seven

SENIOR YEAR AT SANTA CLARA

Around the Santa Clara campus it's known as The Fireplace, although it doesn't actually have a fireplace. The simple three-bedroom bungalow was so named because it sits just across Alviso Street from the Santa Clara fire station.

For two of Steve Nash's four years with the Broncos, The Fireplace was the gathering spot for Santa Clara basketball. And as he worked his way through a pressure-packed senior year, Steve shared those digs with teammates Drew Zurek, Jason Sedlock, Kevin Dunne, Matt Coleman, longtime Victoria friend Brent McLay and assorted other campus characters.

There was no mistaking The Fireplace for anything other than a college basketball crash pad. On the main wall of the spacious but barely-furnished living room was a gigantic promotional banner for the hoops movie "Blue Chips", complete with an image of Shaquille O'Neal flying prone toward one of his monster jams. Other walls were festooned with banners lifted from various Bronco tournament sites — CBS Sports, ESPN Sports Center and that familiar black circle embossed with the four golden letters, N-C-A-A.

While The Fireplace was home to some of Santa Clara's most high-profile student athletes, it was also a typical crash pad for college kids. Cleanliness might be next to Godliness, but don't try to sell that motto to five young men with basketball on the brain. Suffice to say that the constant clutter at The Fireplace should have earned it the nickname The Fire Hazard. Only with each player chipping in a few bucks occasionally for two hours worth of a brave maid's finest work did the house remain in somewhat inhabitable condition.

On Super Bowl Sunday of Steve Nash's senior year, at least half the Bronco basketball team and their friends gathered in the living room of The Fireplace. There was no practice that day. A few of the guys had collected enough money to order 200 chicken wings. One of the two fridges in the kitchen was fairly well-stocked with beer and assorted other beverages. And at half-time, the main TV was quickly turned to Beavis and Butthead's Super Bowl show rather than the overblown Diana Ross extravaganza being offered up by NBC.

It was actually half-time before Steve arrived back at the house after dropping off his visiting mother at the San Jose airport. Seeing no soft place to sit in the crowded living room, he sought out the secondary TV near the kitchen, sprawled out on the empty sofa and closed his eyes. Senior year was beginning to take its toll.

Three days later, those 200 chicken bones were still in residence at The Fireplace, lying vanquished in their Styrofoam containers. The residual smell wasn't pleasant as Steve searched for something to eat in one of the house fridges. "Better stick to the cafeteria food," he said as he carefully eyed a three-day-old sandwich before heading off to class.

Day-to-day life brought a hectic pace for any member of the Santa Clara basketball team. Besides classes and occasionally cramming for an exam or finishing a paper, there was at least two hours of practice a day and a travel schedule that took the Broncos out of town every second weekend of the regular season and often across the country for out-of-conference action.

By the time the mid-way point of his senior year rolled around, Steve Nash was handling the normal student athlete load, as well as a myriad of time-consuming distractions that go along with being a projected NBA first-rounder from a small school. While most of his teammates headed home, to the Benson Center to eat or to class after practice, Steve usually had to wind his way toward the office of Santa Clara sports information director Jim Young, located in a house trailer behind Toso Pavilion. Once there, Steve would do one or two telephone interviews, autograph a few pictures or programs and pick up his fan mail, which by now was arriving daily from all over the U.S. and Canada. To somebody unfamiliar with the hassles of fame, that might not sound like much to deal with, but Steve was often still at Toso a full two hours after the rest of his teammates had left.

When he finally returned to The Fireplace, Steve usually had mail or phone messages waiting. Although he had tried to keep his home number secret to all but a few reporters, there was often a request for yet another interview on the board by the kitchen phone. And on many days, there was a fresh piece of mail from yet another sports agent.

More so than in his previous three seasons, senior year seemed to be a constant struggle for Steve to get enough sleep, eat properly, practise, get homework done and get to class. There just never seemed to be enough time.

With such a whirlwind constantly surrounding him, Steve still felt most comfortable on the basketball court, where decisions had always come easily. And nowhere did he feel more comfortable than at Toso Pavilion, the Broncos' homecourt.

The best word to describe Toso is "quirky". How many other college basketball facilities feature an indoor garden with lush foliage growing in full view from the stands?

Opened in 1975, Toso is covered by a white, air-supported dome that is held in place by the force of 11 fans, making it sort of a mini version of Vancouver's B.C. Place Stadium. On the outside, the building resembles a bunker, partially sunk into the ground on one corner of the Santa Clara campus. On the inside, it's like sitting within a gigantic, hollow marshmallow.

Toso is busy every day, with joggers circling the indoor running track that rings the top of the stadium, and fitness buffs working out on the weights and exercise equipment located behind the stands. It is also the home of the Santa Clara women's volleyball program and, just outside the gym, sits the Broncos' tidy baseball stadium.

With room for about 5,000 fans, Toso is smallish by major U.S. college basketball standards. But it is a building which suits its team — rather quaint and often home to some hair-raising hoops. During Bronco games in Steve's senior year, deafening chants of "S-C-U, S-C-U" emanated from the student section on the baseline. Bronco boosters waved long, coloured

Steve Nash's outstanding outside touch helped to spur a Bronco basketball revival and bring fans out to Toso Pavilion.

balloons to distract opposing shooters and the student band pumped out lively rock songs.

Juxtaposed with the rich history of the Santa Clara men's basketball program — the 1952 Final Four banner that hangs in Toso being the most overt evidence — were the rowdy student fans with their drums and their painted faces who kept themselves busy beating on the inflatable referees they carried into the stands. Not to mention the Broncos' mascot, Bucky, a happy-go-lucky horse in hightops handing out nightly prizes from a fast-food franchise called Cluck U Chicken.

It's hard to pinpoint exactly when it happened. But sometime between the day he arrived as a skinny freshman on Santa Clara's picturesque campus and the start of his senior year, Steve Nash had made Toso Pavilion his house. By the midway point of his senior season, crowds were regularly approaching 5,000 in the building for the first time in years. And when Toso sold out, and Steve was bringing the ball downcourt for Santa Clara, it was an exciting place to be. Bronco basketball was back in the Bay Area and Steve Nash was certainly the man in the middle of that revival.

Nevertheless, a much-anticipated senior season was proving to be a bit of a roller coaster ride for the Broncos and their star point guard. On the court, Santa Clara was winning most of its games. But Steve's numbers were down from his stellar junior season and the team had suffered through some disappointing performances in December.

After beating UCLA in November in Maui, and then cracking the Associated Press Top 25 poll for the first time in 23 seasons, Santa Clara had been riding an incredible wave. Steve Nash had

Passing fancy: Steve Nash served up plenty of sweet dishes for his Santa Clara teammates.

been at the crest of it, rolling up what would stand as a NCAA season-high 15 assists during a 98-59 thrashing of visiting Southern University on December 9. Three days later, Steve shot a chilly two-for-13 from the field against Jerry Tarkanian's Fresno State Bulldogs but dished out 11 assists as the Broncos won 66-58. "Nash beats you any way he wants to," Tark said after the game.

As the Broncos climbed into the national number 22 ranking on December 11, they were being held up as an example of everything good about college sport. "Santa Clara is the cozy little downtown dime store, hanging on for dear life against the mammoth Wal-Marts that have taken over the landscape," wrote columnist Mark Purdy in the San Jose *Mercury News*. "The poll merely shows what basketball insiders have known for some time: Santa Clara, a Catholic school of 3,700 undergraduates, is a statement of stature for college basketball. For everything right about it. For everything possible within it," wrote Adrian Wojnarowski, a columnist with the Fresno *Bee*.

But Steve was well aware that despite their perch in the polls, the Broncos were just one loss away from a quick exit. And that loss would come just five days later, in front of 9,098 fans and 13 NBA scouts at the Mecca Arena in Milwaukee, as Santa Clara was pounded 78-49 by the Marquette Golden Eagles.

Marquette would be the first team that season to effectively throw a blanket over Steve Nash, holding him to just six field-goal attempts, 11 points and four assists. Two nights later, however, Steve bounced back with a 20-point, eight-assist effort as the Broncos salvaged the road trip with an 80-78 squeaker over the Illinois State Redbirds in front of 7,883 fans at Normal, Illinois.

The loss to Marquette was enough to knock the Broncos out of the Top 25 for the remainder of the season. And what followed during the rest of December hadn't been much better.

After barely beating University of the Pacific 75-70 at Toso on December 22, the Broncos took their Christmas break, looking forward to a return seven days later and a matchup with Penn State in the opening round of their own Cable Car Classic tournament in the San Jose Arena.

The Cable Car field was an exceptionally good one this time around. On the other side of the

The Cable Car Classic at the San Jose Arena offered Steve Nash the challenge of guarding Georgia Tech freshman point guard Stephon Marbury.

four-team draw were Bradley University and Georgia Tech. And everyone seemed to be looking forward to a championship game between Santa Clara and Tech that would pit Steve Nash against the Yellow Jackets' freshman point guard sensation Stephon Marbury.

Marbury, a New York city schoolboy legend, had been deemed so valuable to Georgia Tech that he had been flown into Atlanta by Learjet for his recruiting visit to the Yellow Jackets. Even though it was only December, there was already heavy speculation that the freshman might not spend more than a single season in the college ranks before jumping to the NBA. Twenty scouts and four GMs were accredited for the Cable Car tournament in the hopes they would witness a rare Marbury-Nash showdown in the final.

Things didn't go according to form, however, as the Broncos played one of their worst games of the year, losing 70-49 to an undefeated and under-rated Penn State team. Steve was held to just six points by the smothering Nittany Lions' defence and Santa Clara shot a pitiful 30 per cent from the field as a team.

The saving grace as far as the Broncos and Steve Nash were concerned was the fact that Georgia Tech also faltered in its first-round game, losing to Bradley. So Tech and the Broncos and Nash and Marbury would get to meet after all, in the consolation game.

It was a game that would pay off down the line for the Broncos as they outlasted the highly-regarded Yellow Jackets 71-66 in front of 7,802 fans. It would also pay off for Steve Nash, considering he was given the personal decision over Marbury by many observers of the matchup.

Stephon Marbury keeps an eye on his point guard adversary, Broncos' star Steve Nash.

"Steve Nash won the battle of the point guards Saturday night ..." wrote Ron Bergman of the *Mercury News.*

Despite taking a nasty spill on the slippery arena floor in the dying minutes of the game, Steve turned in a solid nine-point, seven-assist performance against Marbury. The Tech freshman finished with a game-high 22 points but managed only four assists and didn't beat Nash cleanly in a one-on-one situation.

"This wasn't a one-on-one game," Steve told the *Mercury News* after it was over. "If it was, I would have scored more points."

"He doesn't have to score," Marbury agreed, referring to Nash. "He's a great leader."

Dick Davey had certainly liked what he'd seen from his vantage point on the Santa Clara bench. Steve Nash, a kid who hadn't been recruited by anybody except Santa Clara, had just out-duelled a consensus top-five NBA draft pick.

Even though he wasn't completely healthy, Steve had created some problems for Marbury one-on-one. For Dick Davey, the game marked the turning point between thinking Steve Nash could be successful at the next level and really knowing it.

The Broncos' roller-coaster ride continued in January with the low point coming during a shocking 72-69 homecourt loss to the last-place Pepperdine Waves. It had been a particularly tough night for Steve, who missed a 17-footer with 18 seconds remaining that would have given the Broncos the lead.

"There are no guarantees any night out with us," Dick Davey said, summing things up succinctly. "We have to play well to win. People are coming in and playing us hard. We have to get over a pretty big hurdle every night."

Nobody had to clear a larger hurdle on a nightly basis than Steve Nash and the statistics reflected that. Steve's numbers were down significantly from his junior season. He was averaging five points and half an assist less per game and his three-point percentage was well below that of the previous season.

But what many people failed to take into account was the special attention Steve was now receiving from every opponent. After his junior year and the *Sports Illustrated* story, he was a marked man. In fact, teams double-teamed him regularly. They used box-and-one and other defences specifically designed to shut him down. Steve was being held, elbowed, tripped and even punched as he fought to get open. Wherever he went, he had a shadow.

"People look at the newspaper and they see me with 11 points, nine points, six points," Steve said, alluding to some of his lower outputs, "but they don't realize that other teams are doing the best they can to take me out of the game. That's one thing I've had to come to grips with this year. But I'm getting used to that. It's a challenge and, hopefully, it'll make me a better player in the long run."

Often though, the special attention meant Steve had to be content with playing the role of decoy, using the focus placed on him to get his teammates open shots. That was fine when they made those shots and when the Broncos were winning. Other times, however, it was frustrating.

In his first three years at Santa Clara, Steve had always managed to get consistent looks at the basket. Suddenly, defences were taking away those looks. More of his shots were coming off the dribble and they came in an erratic cadence. At times, he struggled to find his rhythm.

"I'm kind of shocked when I get an open look sometimes," he admitted, "and I might rush or shuffle my feet a little bit or just get a little bit off-balance. So I've been trying to work really hard so that I can get my game over the hump for this new challenge."

Steve Nash's work didn't end at games or practice, either. Even though he was a star senior winding down his NCAA career, he was often still in Toso well after the gym had closed for the night. There he and Jason Sedlock would play two-on-two or one-on-one, often with friends or with reserve freshmen. Every minute in the gym, Steve reasoned, would pay off.

Something he could not work his way out of, however, was a series of nagging injuries that had slowed him during his senior year. A deep thigh bruise, a pulled hamstring, a sore foot — all these things combined to make it even more difficult to cope with the special defences he was seeing.

With a first-place showdown looming at the University of San Francisco's Memorial Gymnasium on February 1, Steve was averaging just 16 points per game, well under the 20.9 of his junior season. The Broncos, meanwhile, were 13-5 overall but just 4-2 in West Coast Conference play.

Dick Davey had already talked with Steve once or twice about how he was handling the great expectations of his senior year. Davey encouraged Steve to keep shooting, even if they weren't dropping like they had the previous winter. "Hey, you just need to play," the coach told his star player. "Just play your game and the rest will take care of itself."

It was difficult for Steve not to think about the row of NBA scouts who were now at every Santa Clara game. But he had to tell himself that these scouts knew basketball was much more than just the numbers a player posted. And besides, they weren't looking at him to be a scorer. They wanted to see how he ran a team, how he led a team. This Bronco team was an interesting setting in which to evaluate Steve Nash.

"I would say Steve is probably, in a sense, better than he was last year because of the adversity that he's had to go through," Dick Davey said after a mid-season practice.

"I wish I had a better handle on how he is handling all this. All I can say is what he tells me. He's pretty candid in that, at times, maybe all the attention gets a little more than he wants. But he has a dream and in order to fulfill that dream, part of it includes the hype that's involved with the situation. I know he's focused to a certain extent on looking ahead. I'd like to think he still has the interest of the team first and I think he's been very good about that over the years."

"He's so unselfish, you know, almost to a fault sometimes," Davey added. "You'd like to have him be a little bit more selfish, but at the same time, you know how the players feel about him. They love him.

"You get a lot of situations where you get a superstar somewhere and there's a lot of animosity and jealousy with regards to him. Steve doesn't have that here."

"The more attention he gets is great because we're his friends and we want to see him do well, at this level and the next level," agreed teammate Adam Anderson.

Nevertheless, senior year was definitely shaping up to be a learning experience for Steve Nash.

"Now the hype surrounding me, the attention has reached an all-time high," he said as the Broncos prepared to meet USF. "Now everyone's really looking at me because of the talk of the NBA. Everyone wants to be a critic and a coach."

Steve Nash flashed an easy smile as he stood in the driveway of The Fireplace with a cool post-game beer in his hand. He could afford to smile. He had just experienced a night that any college basketball player would have killed for. It had come in a crucial game for the Santa Clara Broncos. And it had come at the expense of the San Francisco Dons.

The Santa Clara-USF matchup came at the half-way point of the Broncos' WCC season. Bay Area papers were heralding it as a true sign of a hoops revival at USF, a school that was making a comeback in basketball after going without a program for three years during the early '80s.

The game was also a showdown for first place in the WCC, with each team sporting a 4-2 conference record before tip-off. And it matched up two star backcourt players in Steve Nash and USF's Gerald Walker, a tremendous athlete who was capable of jumping out of the gym.

By game time, it was also a sellout, as 5,300 fans tried to make their way into creaky Memorial Gymnasium, a building which more closely resembles an old hockey barn in a Canadian prairie town than the sparkling new arenas that many U.S. college basketball teams play in today.

But this old gym was also dripping with history and hoops tradition. On the wall hung the retired green-and-gold numbers of legendary USF stars of the past — Bill Russell's number six, the number four of K.C. Jones and Bill Cartwright's number 24. Among the banners still hanging were two NCAA championship flags, from '55 and '56, when Russell and Jones ruled the Bay Area. In the lobby were bronze plaques, honoring the school's greatest stars.

One new banner in the gym read simply: "This is our house." But on this night it most certainly wasn't. It was pure Nash-ville.

With a half-dozen members of the Toronto Raptors and former Canadian first-round NBA draft choice Leo Rautins in the gym, Steve served up one of his vintage big games. It was a strong effort for the entire Bronco team, but Nash had completely taken it over during one 53-second stretch of the opening half.

With the Broncos up 28-20 and 3:50 remaining, Nash nailed a three from well beyond the arc. After a USF turnover, Steve streaked around a screen just 31 seconds later and buried another three.

Then Steve proceeded to turn in the play of the game. With the speedy Walker on him tightly, Nash froze the USF defender with a between-the-legs dribble that sent Walker stumbling backward. Steve then calmly stepped back and canned another three. There it was, nine points in less than a minute.

Game, set, match to the Broncos.

Or so it should have been. Despite taking a 43-25 lead early in the second half, the Broncos allowed USF a 10-0 run, forcing Steve to take matters into his own hands once again. When the Dons twice cut the lead to eight, Nash responded with a pair of pumping drives through the key for crucial buckets. He sealed matters with another three from the wing with 9:50 remaining.

The final line was impressive. Steve finished with 27 points on ten-for-13 shooting. He was five-for-eight from long distance and he also added five assists. The only thing he hadn't done was pop the popcorn. As he left the 70-57 victory

Steve Nash salutes the crowd in celebration of another great performance. He was a fan favourite during his senior year at Santa Clara.

with 1:12 left, he signalled to the Santa Clara student fans behind the basket. Everybody in that gym, regardless of their affiliation, realized they had witnessed a special performance that night.

It is impossible for most people to relate to Steve Nash's experience as a college senior. He was easily the most identifiable student on campus, yet he was still relatively low-key. He didn't wear flashy clothes or drive a fancy car. In fact, Steve Nash didn't even have a car. He was a celebrity, although he didn't act like one. But as he and his friends cruised the campus area on Saturday nights, they were admitted to any party no matter how crowded. Everybody wanted to fill Steve

Nash's glass, everybody wanted to take care of his friends.

"I do feel more comfortable with all this attention now because I'm an older person, I'm more mature, I can deal with things," Steve told a visiting friend from Victoria.

"I used to hate it when people on campus talked about me. People who didn't even know me would say things like: 'Oh, he's a jerk, he's this, he's that.' You'd hear so many rumours about yourself."

"That was difficult, being 19 or 20 and hearing stuff about yourself when you'd never even been out of your room for most of the year," Steve added. "But now I just take things for what they are. If someone says something about me, I understand why, and I think people probably understand me more around campus these days because I don't try to be someone better than anyone else. You know, I'm pretty regular. That's the way I grew up. I grew up very average."

A few hours after this conversation, Steve Nash was once again living an experience that was anything but average. A sell-out crowd of 5,000 had packed Toso to see the team's rematch with USF. The Mavericks, Magic, Bullets and Clippers were there, too.

Once again, Steve didn't shoot particularly well, going 4-for-12 from the field. But he played a major role in a swarming Broncos' defence that completely dominated USF during a 65-41 victory.

"They are to be congratulated for just kicking the crap out of us," said USF coach Phil Mathews afterward. "I'm not even going to watch this game film. It's so bad I'll probably burn it."

While Mathews was talking after the game, the entire Broncos team was sitting along the scorer's table on their homecourt. It was Autograph Night and fans were lining up to have Santa Clara players sign a team picture. One lineup snaked left and down the side of the court, waiting for all but one of the Broncos to sign. The other one snaked right and all the way around the back of the bleachers.

That lineup was for Steve Nash.

A short walk from Toso Pavilion is the Santa Clara University bookstore. On one rack in that outlet during Steve's senior season hung a row of pricey Broncos basketball jerseys, bearing the number 11. That particular jersey was there because Steve had made the number popular enough to sell, yet he received not a dime of the profits.

It was a small example of the inequity of the NCAA, the organization which governs U.S. college sports. According to the rules, which are broken across the country every day of every season, college athletes can't be paid. They are allowed to receive only books, tuition, accommodation and meals from the university for which they play. Meanwhile, the NCAA reaps millions of dollars yearly from basketball TV revenue and a growing list of secondary sources.

As Steve Nash completed his senior year at Santa Clara, he had developed some strong opinions on this subject. In fact, parts of his senior thesis dealt with the way the NCAA operates as a cartel, enjoying a rather unethical monopoly and thus being able to exploit its student-athletes.

"I think there should be more compensation for the athletes' participation," Steve said. "And I think they should guard against players being exploited. The NCAA guards against everything else. Why can't they protect the players as well?"

Proponents of athletes' rights believe that the NCAA should at the very least pool money made from things such as souvenir sales into a fund for players to draw from after they have exhausted their college eligibility. Others believe that athletes should receive an allowance, so that schools and boosters wouldn't be tempted to break the rules. In an age when the Olympics have admitted professional athletes, the "shamateurism" of the NCAA smacks of hypocrisy.

"By NCAA rules, an athlete can't have a job during the school year [or money earned is deducted from scholarship funds]. What happens from March to June when he has no extra money?" Steve pointed out. "When they're not playing, they can't work. I think that's unfair. There should be some compensation made. What happens to the kids whose families don't have any money? They have to pay for the kid to get to school and then there's no money for the kid to buy detergent or clothes or go to the movies."

Steve's thesis pointed out how an athletic scholarship and the athlete's privileges within that scholarship, are essentially the same today as in 1950. Meanwhile, the revenue generated by NCAA basketball has escalated by enormous proportions. In 1995, CBS agreed to a new $1.725-billion US contract to televise the NCAA Tournament through the year 2002. Each game played in the 1996 Tournament paid $60,400 per team to the participating teams' conferences.

"It really is a cartel," Steve said. "It's a restrictive earnings monopoly. The NCAA controls everything and they allow no-one else to enter into the marketplace. There's no competitor, there's no opposition."

Because of the system, it is doubtful that athletes will ever band together to change the rules in their favour, however.

"The kids are 19 when they come to college. If they're going to join forces and battle the NCAA, they could be risking giving up these four precious years of their life," Steve said. "They're taking a chance. And the freshman are going to have to say right away: 'OK, yes, we're being exploited', when they're not really educated about that. So it's a situation where the NCAA knows that the athletes really can't provide an opposition to their methods and is exploiting the athletes and taking advantage of them because of that."

Unlike most of the other athletes at Santa Clara, Steve Nash had some extra income during his four years of college basketball. By playing for the Canadian national team, he earned about $2,000 per summer, a figure he described as "pretty decent".

"But I can't do the things that some of the other kids here do," he said, pointing around the relatively wealthy Santa Clara campus, dotted with Mercedes and BMWs. "I can't go to Reno and Tahoe all the time and I don't have a car. I don't have money to go away on weekends."

Of course it seems ludicrous that, with one hand, the NCAA makes money off the backs of its athletes while, with the other, it penalizes these same athletes for the most minor rules infractions. A few weeks after this discussion, Steve picked up a newspaper to learn that Villanova all-American Kerry Kittles had been handed a three-game suspension by the NCAA. His crime? Charging personal phone calls to a university credit card number.

Tucked away in the hills of tiny Moraga, seemingly a world away from the urban mass of the Bay Area, is the campus of Saint Mary's College. It is a welcome escape from the teeming cities of Oakland, San Francisco and San Jose right next door, a quiet country respite.

But when Saint Mary's and Santa Clara hook up for a basketball game, the Gaels' home gym is anything but quiet. The two Bay Area private schools have been arch rivals for the 70 years that they have been playing hoops.

During his four seasons with the Broncos, Steve Nash had always looked forward to visiting Saint Mary's, where the fans got on his case early and often. And as Steve visited McKeon Pavilion for the last time on February 14, the Saint Mary's crew was waiting for him.

The gym was jammed with 3,212 fans. Some students clutched gigantic hearts and each other's hands, obviously making a Valentine's Day date out of the big game. They would be anything but sweet to the Broncos' star point guard, however.

Steve trotted onto the court with a freshly-shaved head, his usual baggy shorts and white warm-up top hanging loosely off his body as he drained three after three in warm-up. The rabid Saint Mary's student section would be on him all night, spurred on by the Gaels' cartoon-like mascot wearing the oversized helmet and plume of an Irish knight.

"Canada sucks!" yelled one loud student in the Saint Mary's section, pretty much setting the tone for the night.

"You're going to the Clippers, Nash!," yelled another.

Actually, the Clippers — the traditional NBA doormat — weren't there. The Bullets were the only NBA team represented on press row this night. But more important to Steve was the presence of his brother Martin, and the rest of the Canadian Olympic soccer team which, by coincidence, was training and playing in the Bay Area.

Martin and the lads had made their way to the game dressed in their Olympic team track suits. In the hostile Gaels' gym, they would serve as a nice bit of counter-balance for the Broncos.

Steve put on an incredible show for his countrymen, hitting his first four shots and scoring 13 of the Broncos' first 17 points in the game's opening five minutes. Nobody on the Gaels could guard him as he drained three three-pointers to get the Broncos off to a lead they would never relinquish. By half-time, Steve had 17 points and the Broncos led 42-28. Almost single-handedly, he had defused this 70-year-old roundball rivalry.

As the Saint Mary's hopes faded in the second half, a fellow who had painted his entire face Gael blue for the game began a chant: "B-O-B-B-Y H-U-R-L-E-Y!" he shouted at Steve, in a derisive comparison to the Sacramento point guard. When that didn't catch on, he began another chant: "C-B-A, C-B-A!", suggesting that Steve was headed for the Continental Basketball Association, basketball's minor leagues.

Steve would eventually cool off, making just one of his final 11 shots to finish with 22 points on six-for-18 shooting, along with five assists. But he had done all the damage he needed to do during the first five minutes and Santa Clara cruised to a 79-65 final.

"He makes me look a lot better than I am. I know that," Dick Davey said during the post-game press conference. "He takes over games and when he does, you just enjoy it."

Saint Mary's coach Ernie Kent could only agree.

"You've really got to tip your hat to him," Kent said of Steve. "He gets fired up with a big rivalry like this. He just put us in a hole by himself to start the game."

Four days later, Santa Clara and Saint Mary's resumed their rivalry on a special afternoon in Toso Pavilion.

It was Seniors Day, a traditional time when graduating Broncos are honoured before the final regular-season home game of their careers. But there would be an added musical twist to the pre-game ceremony on this particular Seniors Day.

Dennis Leach, who normally sings the Canadian anthem before San Jose Sharks National Hockey League home games, was enlisted by Santa Clara to perform "O Canada" before the game in honour of graduating Canadian imports Steve Nash and Brendan Graves. A taped rendition of the French anthem was also played in honour of fellow senior Phil Von Buchwaldt, a

Jean and John Nash pose with the Broncos' mascot Bucky prior to taking the court for Seniors' Day ceremonies at Toso.

likable six-foot-eleven import who teammates joked had learned all his English during the past four years from watching ESPN.

With the Canadian flag raised beside the Stars and Stripes on this afternoon, Steve and Brendan flashed huge grins at each other. With their families included in the sold-out crowd of more than 5,000, this was an afternoon neither would ever forget.

On the court things didn't go quite as smoothly for Steve Nash and the Broncos, however. Plagued by early foul trouble after a minor altercation with the Gaels' Josh Unruh, Steve was limited to 29 minutes in a too-close-for-comfort 64-61 Santa Clara win. He ended up scoring 21 points, but shot just seven-for-20 in his final regular-season game at Toso.

"It was a nice day before the game started. Then it got ugly," said a somber Steve, who had felt dizzy at the line late in the game when he uncharacteristically missed two free throws.

Nevertheless, it was a day to pay tribute to what Steve had accomplished during four years at Toso. He had been introduced as Santa Clara's "all-time great" during pre-game introductions and one off-day wasn't going to change anybody's opinion.

"He's a great player," said Saint Mary's coach Ernie Kent. "He's ready for the next level and I wish him very well going there. I think he's been terrific for their program and for our league."

Steve Nash wasn't feeling so terrific a few days later, however. The Broncos were in the midst of a crucial two-game northern road trip to end their WCC regular season. The trip had begun horribly in Portland.

It was likely Steve's worst game of his senior season as Portland's Dionn Holton scored 17 and held the Broncos' point guard to just eight points on four-of-12 shooting in an 80-71 loss. Santa Clara trailed by as many as 19 points during a defeat which would cost them a shot at the outright WCC regular-season title. Steve committed six turnovers in the loss and, for one of the few times in his career, struggled while trying to break fullcourt pressure.

"He [Nash] didn't play well at all," Dick Davey told the San Francisco *Chronicle* afterward, "He was just one of the boys out there."

Steve's performance added to a late-season shooting slump that had seen him make just 13 of his last 48 shots and only one of his last 15 three-point attempts.

That night, Steve sounded depressed on the phone to his mother, Jean, back in Victoria. "Mom, I'm sure the scouts are not interested in me anymore after this," he said. "But it doesn't matter. I'm still going to make the NBA."

He didn't have to wait long for his chance at redemption. Just two nights later, Steve Nash rebounded with one of his best performances as a Bronco in one of his team's most important games.

Despite their loss to Portland, the Broncos rolled into Spokane with a chance to tie the Gonzaga Bulldogs for the conference regular-season title. Santa Clara was 9-4 while the Bulldogs were 10-3. A Broncos' victory would see the teams end the season deadlocked. And since Santa Clara had won their first meeting, 72-61 back at Toso in January, the Broncos also still had a chance to lock up top seed for the WCC post-season tournament.

Anybody who has played there, however, knows a victory at Gonzaga's Martin Centre, a shoebox of a gym where the decibel level can easily go through the roof, is anything but routine. Still, the Broncos had enjoyed much more than average success there with Steve Nash running the show. Bulldogs fans remembered well that, just a year earlier, Steve had pumped in 40 points as Santa Clara snapped a 34-game Zags' home-court winning streak.

This time, Gonzaga took a 17-game home streak into the showdown in front of 4,100 fans. The game had been sold out for a week and the Kennel Club, a group of about 100 of the noisiest fans in college basketball, was primed and growling for this one.

Unfortunately for the Bulldogs, so were Steve

Nash and his teammates. With the regular season on the line, Steve scored 24 points and added six assists and four rebounds as Santa Clara clinched a share of first place with a 77-71 victory. Backcourt mate Marlon Garnett also came up big, sinking all but two of his 18 points in the second half including a three-pointer that broke a 64-64 tie with 3:38 remaining.

Steve contributed a late jumper and two free throws with a second left to ice the crucial win. As he left the game, he raised his arms in victory and, addressing the Gonzaga student section, pointed to his jersey and grinned.

That clutch performance certainly didn't hurt a few days later as WCC coaches voted on the conference player-of-the-year award. Despite his numbers being down significantly from his junior year, Steve earned the MVP honour for the second straight season. He was only the eleventh player in conference history to win the award twice. But Steve knew he would gladly trade in that hardware for some serious success in the post-season.

That post-season would begin a week later at Toso Pavilion on a glorious spring day. The sun shone across the steps of the Santa Clara stadium as hotdogs and chicken burgers sizzled on an outdoor grill and fans lined up from the ticket booth window well back into the parking lot.

This was an exciting time for everybody connected with the league. The WCC Tournament represented a rebirth for all eight conference teams. It was a three-day, single-knockout format that would send one winner on to the NCAA Tournament.

The Broncos didn't play their opener against Pepperdine until 6 p.m. but Steve Nash and several of his teammates showed up at Toso early in the afternoon to watch the other opening-round games. Damian Grant, a former high school teammate of Steve's who had been sleeping on the couch of The Fireplace for most of senior year, had also developed an entrepreneurial streak. Grant was selling his own version of the Santa Clara playoff t-shirt. And as Steve sat by his Victoria buddy autographing the t-shirts for whoever bought them, business was booming.

By the time the Broncos' game arrived, the upper reaches of Toso were overflowing. Fans were eager to see Steve Nash lead Santa Clara into the Big Dance in his last weekend ever on the Toso floor.

History was definitely against the Broncos, however. In each of the nine previous conference tournaments, the host school had failed to win. The Broncos had won nine of ten games at Toso that season but their only loss had come, strangely enough, to last-place Pepperdine. Now, in their first game of the WCC tournament, Pepperdine was once again the opponent.

Still, nobody expected a repeat of that stunning January upset, least of all the 20 NBA scouts who had been accredited for the WCC Tournament, many of them there to evaluate Steve Nash. Pepperdine entered the tournament with a 9-17 record and had lost eight straight games to end the regular season. The Waves had seen their head coach resign in mid-January and, to make matters worse, they were down to just eight players on the bench as their nightmare season neared its completion.

It appeared as though the nightmare would continue as the Broncos took a quick seven-point lead to start the game. And it seemed all but over when Pepperdine then lost WCC scoring leader Gerald Brown to a knee injury after a late first-half collision with teammate Bryan Hill. Hill also went to the dressing room for the rest of the first half with a severe headache.

But it was the Broncos who would end the night needing Extra Strength Tylenol. The freak first-half accident seemed to strangely motivate the shorthanded Waves, who took over the game from that point on.

Steve Nash sensed that Pepperdine had become instantly energized by the turn of events: "When their coach quit, they came in here and beat us," he stressed to his teammates during a time-out. "Do you think they'll back down now?"

Santa Clara had been up 23-22 when the collision occurred. But by halftime, the Broncos trailed 29-25. They would lead only once briefly in the second half, when Steve buried a three-pointer from the wing with 4:30 left.

The Waves, shooting well and playing aggressive defence, managed to hang on down the stretch. On the final play of the game, Steve brought the ball up-court with the Broncos needing a three-pointer to tie. Double-teamed as he crossed the midcourt line, he dished to Kevin Dunne, who kicked it to Lloyd Pierce. But Pierce's open three from the left corner missed as the horn sounded. Pepperdine had scored an unbelievable 63-60 upset.

"Sure I would have liked to shoot it," Steve would say later about the game's final play. "But I thought afterwards how would I feel in case I missed it when I took a 30-footer with two guys on me, one of them a six-foot-seven athlete? We've got good players on the court. We got a good shot, so I can't really second-guess what happened. I think it's just unfortunate the ball didn't go in."

The Toso faithful were stunned. For the second straight spring, their top-seeded Broncos had been upended by the WCC's last-place team.

To make matters worse, this was also the last time most of them would see Steve Nash in a college uniform. Individually, it had been an outstanding performance for Nash, who finished with 25 points on nine-for-16 shooting, including a brilliant seven-for-ten from three-point range. The rest of the Broncos had shot a combined 14-for-47, however, and had missed countless easy chances inside.

It was one of the most disappointing moments in Steve Nash's life and possibly the end of his college career. But instead of heading straight for the locker room, he walked to midcourt and pointed toward the fans in the Toso stands. In the great tradition of English soccer players, Steve raised his hands above his head and clapped them together slowly, saluting the Santa Clara fans who had been so good to him for four years. He then walked to the baseline and repeated the gesture for the Broncos' student section. "English soccer players thank the fans after the game because the fans make the atmosphere and they make the sport what it is with their effort and passion for the game," Steve would explain later about this gesture.

A half-hour after the crushing loss, Steve Nash and Dick Davey filed into the squash court that was serving as an interview room for the WCC Tournament. Steve's eyes were red, his face vacant and tired. The NCAA Tournament, seemingly a lock for Santa Clara even a few hours before, was now in doubt.

"It's tough to say we're in right now, because I'm pretty discouraged," Steve said. "But I really feel we deserve to be there. We had a pretty phenomenal year, considering how people were coming at us from day one and all the pressure people put on us. So, although I'm disappointed, I don't think it's over and I think we still have a chance to make it a special season. I really feel we'll be in two Sundays from now."

When a giant is slain, there is always a giant killer lurking somewhere in the plot. Portland ultimately filled that role as the WCC Tournament concluded two nights later. The Pilots earned their first NCAA berth since 1959 with a 76-68 upset of Gonzaga in the championship game.

The Pilots were in. The Broncos, and Steve Nash, would once again have to wait until Selection Sunday to learn their post-season fate.

their chief WCC rival for an at-large berth. And they had a national-level star in Steve Nash.

But they also had on record their two unfathomable losses to Pepperdine, a school not even ranked among the top 200 in the NCAA. Any way you looked at it, gaining a berth would call for some luck.

"I'm more nervous for this thing this year," Dick Davey confided to the *Chronicle*.

When Selection Sunday finally arrived, CBS made it even more dramatic for the Broncos. The East, Midwest and Southeast brackets were all announced first. And when George Washington was unveiled as the 11th seed in the West, the Broncos' hearts sank. Then, almost magically, Santa Clara's name appeared on the screen, the 61st team announced out of a field of 64. And the Broncos had drawn a decent seed. They were number ten in the West and would meet Maryland that Friday in Tempe, Arizona.

The 25 players and friends gathered at The Fireplace to watch the selection show cheered wildly. For Steve, who had spent the week methodically assessing the Broncos' chances, it was sweet. "It's definitely a relief," he grinned.

The Broncos had a lot going for them as they jockeyed for an at-large berth during the eight days between their first-round WCC loss and Selection Sunday. They boasted an impressive Ratings Performance Index ranking of 33rd in the nation, they had big non-conference wins over UCLA, Michigan State, Georgia Tech and Fresno State to their credit. They had swept Gonzaga,

Santa Clara entered its third NCAA Tournament in four years decidedly on the limp. Kevin Dunne had dislocated a finger, Marlon Garnett was nursing a sore knee and ankle and Adam Anderson had a broken nose. But it was Steve Nash's health that was most troubling to Dick Davey.

A sore left hamstring kept Steve out of the

Broncos' open practice during their first day at Arizona State's University Activity Center. While his teammates ran through a series of light drills in the cozy, 14,198-seat facility, Steve stood on the sideline bouncing a ball and occasionally stretching or taking treatment on his hamstring.

It was the first question at the post-practice press conference, which attracted about 40 reporters. As Steve sat with Dick Davey and Marlon Garnett at the long table covered with blue bunting and NCAA logos, he addressed questions about his health.

"It's just nagging injuries, nothing major," Steve maintained. "We just thought it was better to take it easy today so I can go at full strength tomorrow."

Truth be known, the injury was a worry for Steve and the Broncos. They would need their point guard at his best if they had any hope of breaking Maryland's ferocious full-court press. The Terrapins, 17-12 despite a tough Atlantic Coast Conference schedule, were dearly missing post Joe Smith who had jumped to the NBA the previous season. But they could still pressure teams better than almost anybody in the country. Any injury that would slow Steve Nash was a concern for Santa Clara.

Meanwhile, Maryland coach Gary Williams spent much of his press conference explaining why his program hadn't recruited Steve Nash out of high school. His players talked about how they would need solid team defence to contain Nash. Nobody was overlooking him or the Broncos.

"We're well aware of Santa Clara, especially the guard Steve Nash," said Terrapin forward Keith Booth. "We get ESPN on the East Coast as well."

Williams drew a comparison between Nash and his former star Joe Smith, who had led the Terps to the Sweet Sixteen the previous season before being drafted, number one overall, by the Golden State Warriors.

"Those guys kind of pull the program with them," said the Maryland coach. "They give people confidence who play with them, they attract other people — not just with their basketball ability but with the charisma they give off. Those guys are fun to play with. Without knowing Nash personally, I would say it looks like that's what he gives to that team."

The pre-tournament press conference included plenty of the inevitable "senior" questions, too.

"Steve, not to be negative, but this could be your last game, ever, for the Broncos ..." began a Bay Area reporter.

"Thanks for pointing that out," Steve shot back to laughs around the room.

"Yeah, of course that goes through my mind," he admitted. "But as long as I go out there tomorrow with a smile on my face, having fun, that's the main thing."

The Santa Clara Broncos filed quietly from their bus down the corridor and into their dressing room located in the outer ring of Arizona State's Activity Center. It was one hour before game time.

Ten minutes later, most of the Broncos were out on the shiny hardwood floor, getting a feel for the lighting in the arena and shooting jumpers. Steve Nash, who had been undergoing treatment on his hamstring, was the last player to take the floor. But as the Maryland and Santa Clara pep bands dueled from diagonal sides of the building, Steve was raining threes from well outside the line. Swish, swish, swish. One after another they dropped through the twine.

Although the building wouldn't completely fill up until the evening doubleheader which featured the Arizona Wildcats, the atmosphere was intense by the time the Santa Clara-Maryland matinee tip-off arrived to chants of "S-C-U, S-C-U" from the sizable crowd of boosters who had made the trip to the desert from the Bay Area.

The game would begin on a shaky note for Santa Clara, however. The Maryland press proved to be every bit as suffocating as advertised and it posed some early problems for the Broncos as they coughed up the ball in the onslaught of long arms and quick feet. Steve missed his first two shots from the field and things were going the Terps' way as they took a quick 11-6 lead.

But before the midway point of the first half, Steve and the Broncos seemed to relax and find multiple solutions to the Maryland pressure. Once they broke the press, they began to get some easy buckets in transition.

Not only that, but the Maryland pressure was quickly getting the Terps into foul trouble. Santa Clara found itself in the bonus with 8:58 remaining in the first half. And four straight free throws by Steve to end the half sent the Broncos into the dressing room with a 35-31 lead.

Steve had enjoyed a tremendous first half, breaking the Maryland pressure and dazzling the crowd with his ballhandling and passing skills, racking up ten points and six assists. "He's the Gretzky of the court out there," gushed one

Blowing past defenders such as Exree Hipp, Steve Nash led the Broncos to a 1996 first-round NCAA Tournament upset over Maryland at Tempe, Arizona.

newspaper type in the media room at half-time. "He's a helluva player. They'd be a different team without him," added another.

The determined Terps opened the second half with a five-point run to grab a 36-35 lead. But instead of wilting, Santa Clara bounced back bravely. Steve set up Kevin Dunne with a perfect feed inside to draw a foul and then hit a three from the baseline himself to regain the lead for the Broncos.

A few minutes later came the play that swung the ball game. Marlon Garnett took an assist from Steve to drain a three. On the same play, Bronco forward Drew Zurek was pushed inside by the Terps' Rodney Elliott. Zurek capitalized on the ensuing free throws, giving Santa Clara a six-point bulge with 14:14 left.

Garnett then scored on a backdoor lay-up off another feed from Steve. Adam Anderson canned an open three, Zurek scored inside and Dunne tipped in a miss by Steve. It was a stunning 14-0 Santa Clara run over less than three-and-a-half minutes and it had the Broncos leading 62-47. That was it. Game over. Santa Clara had handed Maryland its only first-round defeat in 13 NCAA Tournament appearances. "This ain't the way I imagined going out," dejected senior Terp forward Mario Lucas would say afterward.

The Terps had no choice in the dying minutes but to foul Steve and he proceeded to salt away the game at the free-throw line. The Broncos won going away, 91-79, as chants of "OVER-RATED" rained down on the Maryland bench.

Steve left the game with 29 seconds remaining. He was beaming, saluting the pro-Santa Clara crowd and pointing to the section where his high school coaches Ian Hyde-Lay, Ted Anderson and Bill Greenwell sat. As Nash plopped down on the bench, a hoarse-voiced Bronco fan yelled out: "STEVE, We love you man!"

Steve would end the game with 28 points, going three-for-four from three-point range and 17-for-18 from the line. He also added 12 assists, which could easily have been 20 had his teammates been able to convert on more of his passes. For good measure, he pulled down six rebounds and made a pair of steals. The banner headline in the following day's San Jose *Mercury News* would read simply: "MONSTER NASH".

After the final buzzer had sounded, Dick Davey and Steve Nash stepped to midcourt for the CBS interview. It was a great victory. But as they faced the camera, the gigantic blue banner of Kansas passed behind them. The mighty Jayhawks, about to dispense of South Carolina State, would be the Broncos' second-round opponent. And that would be another battle altogether.

Long after the rest of the Broncos had been poked and prodded by the fascinated college basketball media, a few dedicated columnists from Denver, Seattle, San Francisco and Victoria were still waiting for Steve Nash to emerge from the NCAA's random drug-testing lab.

"Has Nash peed yet?" Santa Clara sports information director Jim Young asked as he waited outside in the hallway. "He hasn't? He's still in there?"

A few minutes later, Steve emerged, grinning sheepishly. "I needed about six or seven Canadian beer, like Ben Johnson in Seoul," he joked to the remaining writers.

This was a good time for Steve, a relaxing time. He was still having to explain Canada and why he didn't get recruited out of high school to U.S. reporters and columnists. But he was doing it in the locker room after an NCAA Tournament win. He felt so much better than he had just two weeks earlier after the Pepperdine loss.

"Now that it's coming to the end of my career, I want to look back on it and say: 'I had a great time'," Steve said. "I don't want to look back on it and say: 'God, there was a lot of pressure and we didn't do as well as we would have liked'.

"We'd really like to take advantage of the

opportunity and not be happy just being here," he added. "It would have been disappointing to be leaving today."

By the time he had finished all the interviews and the treatment on his hamstring and arrived back at the Phoenix Hyatt, Steve was exhausted. He lay down on his bed and drifted off to sleep. When he awoke, he was horrified to discover that he had slept right through a team meeting.

Dick Davey was steamed. Team meetings were mandatory for everybody. By chance, the Santa Clara head coach passed Ian Hyde-Lay, Steve's high school coach, in the Hyatt lobby. As Hyde-Lay said hello, Davey shot back: "Maybe you'd better get a flight home tomorrow. Your friend might not play Sunday."

Panicking for a second, Hyde-Lay was tempted to run after Davey and try to talk him out of benching Steve. But Hyde-Lay's SMUS assistant, Bill Greenwell, stopped him. "Relax Hydes," he said. "Think about it. It's not going to happen."

Steve wasn't so sure. He stewed about Dick Davey's reaction all evening, wondering what the coach would do. When Davey returned to the hotel, Steve met him immediately, apologizing for missing the meeting. Davey accepted his apology. Nothing more would come of it.

If you were to assemble a list of the great basketball schools in the U.S., Kansas would be in most people's Top Ten. The Jayhawks are one of the truly storied programs in the NCAA and they give off that aura wherever they play.

At Tempe for this Western sub-regional, the nationally fourth-ranked Jayhawks were the "name" team. Their first open practice drew about 2,000 fans, who cheered each drill as if it were a game-winning, last-second basket. Coached by Roy Williams and led by all-American point guard Jacque Vaughn, Kansas had been tabbed by many to advance to the Final Four in East Rutherford.

The Broncos were definite underdogs — 11 points according to the Las Vegas line. Yet there were plenty of people whispering about a possible upset leading up to this Sunday afternoon game which would send the winner on to Regional semifinals the following weekend in Denver.

There were also plenty of people anticipating an exciting showdown between Steve Nash and Jacque Vaughn. The pre-game hype centred almost solely on this matchup. "Nash is a classic, but so is Vaughn," blared the Arizona *Republic* headline. "Maybe, in 15 years or so, there will be another matchup like this one," the story began.

"He's a great leader and I think that's what I respect the most about him," said Steve of Jacque Vaughn as the Broncos prepared for their huge challenge.

"People can sort of glorify the matchup and make it as romantic as you want it to be, but I really don't think it's that big a deal," Steve added. "Hopefully, I can stay with him and show that I can play a little bit. But I could go out tomorrow and Jacque Vaughn could kick my butt and I'll still find something positive out of it. I'll find something I have to work on."

"I don't look at individual matchups," Vaughn countered. "It'll be my team against his team. I'll have the chance to neutralize his game and he'll have the chance to neutralize mine."

While the Vaughn-Nash matchup was the obvious story line, the most popular subplot was still the fact that just about every college in America had passed on Steve coming out of high school. Kansas had turned him down and just about every writer from every city wanted to know if their particular school had, too. "Steve, did you send a letter to Arizona State?" asked a Phoenix writer. "I'm from Denver, did you send a letter to Colorado State?" asked another.

"I'm just one of thousands of kids who sent letters to all those schools and just one of thousands of kids who got turned down by all those schools," Steve said, over and over again, to wave after wave of cameras and microphones. "You know, I never really gave up on myself."

Steve felt loose and happy during an informal team dinner Saturday night at an Italian restaurant in downtown Phoenix, bouncing from table to table to visit, but mostly hanging around the hometown table that included his high school coaches and his mom, Jean.

After dessert, an elderly female Santa Clara booster who was leaving the restaurant with her husband, bent over and kissed him softly on the cheek.

"I hope you can do it tomorrow," she told Steve, "because I might not live long enough to get back to another one of these."

The sun beat down heavily on the Activity Center in the two hours before Sunday's big double-header. The first game was the one locals were there to see — pitting nearby Arizona against Iowa. The second game would feature mighty Kansas against Santa Clara. It was March, but fans rolled up to the arena wearing shades and their shirts wrapped around their waists. Scalpers did a brisk business as walk-ups hunted for tickets wherever they could find them.

As Arizona was wrapping up its berth to Denver with an 87-73 win over the Hawkeyes, Steve sat in the crowd between Marlon Garnett and Jake, a large bottle of Gatorade in one hand. With about six minutes left in the Arizona win, the Broncos filed back to their locker room. Once inside, Dick Davey told his troops: "They have 11 high school all-Americans on their team. We have none. But that doesn't mean anything."

Forty minutes later, Steve Nash trotted through a tunnel of cheerleaders and onto the floor as the arena announcer boomed out his name. He met Jacque Vaughn at halfcourt, patted his adversary on the butt, and lined up for the tip in front of 12,441 fans and the CBS cameras.

That moment was about as good as the afternoon would get, however. For all the upsets the Broncos had pulled during Steve's four-year career, it just wasn't in the cards this time. The Jayhawks were simply too deep and too talented and the Broncos were too flat.

One of the first plays of the game would set the tone for the whole afternoon. Steve Nash fed a wide-open Brendan Graves on the break but, instead of a thundering dunk, Graves bobbled the ball out of bounds.

Kansas' silky-smooth shooting guard Jerod Haase opened the scoring with a three from the baseline a few seconds later. Before the Broncos could catch their breath, the Jayhawks were up

As Steve Nash heads around Jayhawk point guard Jacque Vaughn on the dribble, defender Raef LaFrentz stands waiting. The Broncos met the Jayhawks for Steve's final game as a college player.

12-0. Steve, bothered much more by the sore hamstring than he would let on to anybody, simply couldn't hit. With their star struggling to find his shooting touch, the Broncos had absolutely no chance. They fell behind 20-8 and the game was out of reach before they knew it.

By half-time, Steve had missed all six of his shots and his teammates hadn't fared much better. The Broncos trailed 46-22 heading into the dressing room. About the only thing still at stake was pride.

Jean Nash managed a brave smile as she watched her son run by on the way to the locker room.

"It's pretty tough to come back from down 24, isn't it?" she said.

Pretty impossible, actually, when the opponent is Kansas. The Broncos turned in a solid second-half effort, but they eventually succumbed 76-51. Six-foot-11 forward Raef LaFrentz had been red-hot for the Jayhawks, hitting for 19 points on nine-of-ten shooting, including a perfect seven-for-seven in the first half when the game was decided.

Steve, meanwhile, couldn't have been colder. He missed his first eight shots and his first points of the game didn't come until he hit a pair of free throws with 14:22 remaining in the second half. He and his Broncos teammates hustled and dove all over the court during the final 20 minutes but it wasn't nearly enough to make up such a big deficit against a quality team like Kansas.

As Steve exited his final college game with 4:36 left, the Bronco section in the stadium rose to applaud. "Thank-you, Steve!" bellowed the same hoarse-voiced spectator from two days earlier. A water bottle in hand, Steve took a few deep breaths, draping a towel partially over his face as he looked up toward his Mom in the stands.

Two minutes later, Kevin Dunne came out. He and Steve hugged at the far end of the bench. Marlon Garnett was next. Steve embraced him and rubbed his head. In the background, the Kansas fans droned out their traditional, eerie victory chant. "Rock Chalk, Jayhawk — Kaaaaay Uuuuuu."

"A lot was going through my mind. I'm going out of the game and I'm thinking: 'I'm probably never going to play a college game again'," Steve recalls. "You know, it's sort of a shocking moment and then it sort of keeps hitting you gradually and gradually and it's hard to absorb it all at once."

There was silence and plenty of red eyes as the Broncos made their way back to the dressing room. Steve brought up the rear, talking to a fan. "Hey man, I'm going to call you when you're in the league," the stranger said, "and you can get me tickets."

Back inside the locker room, it was an emotional moment. For five of these players — Kevin Dunne, Phil Von Buchwaldt, Brendan Graves, Adam Anderson and Steve Nash — it was the end of an era. It had all gone by so fast. It had all ended so suddenly. Somebody started to cry. Somebody else began to tell jokes. Fifteen minutes after one of the most disappointing finishes of their careers, most of the Broncos were laughing.

"Obviously, I think all the people here know it was a real clinic by Kansas," Dick Davey told the post-game press conference. "We just couldn't climb that mountain today."

"It was very emotional," Davey continued. "It

was very hard for me to talk to them after the game. Five seniors we're losing and they've been the cornerstone of my four years, obviously, as a head coach. I've been on the coattails of those guys and so now I have to go out and see what coaching is all about."

Much of the post-game analysis, naturally, once again centred around the Steve Nash-Jacque Vaughn matchup. The press had ruled nearly unanimously that Vaughn had dominated. The New York *Times* story said Nash got "lost in a Kansas forest" and certainly Kansas players felt that their man had won. "Jacque is one of the best defensive point guards in the country. I think he made the looks difficult [for Nash]," said forward Scot Pollard. Indeed, the looks had been tough for every Santa Clara player as the Broncos shot 16-for-64 as a team for a dismal 25 per cent, compared to 42 per cent for Kansas.

Steve began the final press conference of his college career by taking the blame for the loss. And despite the fact he had been nearly hobbled by the hamstring all weekend, he refused to use his injury as an excuse.

"I was fine," he said. "For the most part, I just didn't get it done. We really took it on the chin early. I think the key was I just didn't make shots. I got some looks that I would normally knock down and I just didn't knock them down today. I think everybody's had one of those days. It's just disappointing that it had to be my last one."

Certainly, the ultra-quick Vaughn's defence had contributed to Steve's own horrible one-for-11 shooting performance. But what wasn't pointed out by many was the fact Vaughn had plenty of help from his teammates. And in a straight statistical comparison, Steve had actually fared at least as well. He had scored only seven points but Vaughn had managed just two himself on one-for-six shooting. Steve's eight rebounds were three better than his rival's and each player had collected six assists and three steals.

But the media always gets the last word and the fact that one post-game TV report would characterize it as Jacque Vaughn "smoking" Steve Nash didn't do wonders for Steve's morale. Another report said that Vaughn had "turned Stevie Nash into Stevie Nicks." Some of the young, post-Fleetwood Mac Broncos watching the report on television looked at each other blankly. "Who's Stevie Nicks?"

Steve Nash ended his senior season at Santa Clara averaging 17 points, 6 assists and 3.6 rebounds. He was an honourable mention all American selection by both the Associated Press and the U.S. Basketball Writers' Association.

He would exit as Santa Clara's all-time assists leader with 510 despite playing just two seasons at the point. He would also finish as the finest three-point and free-throw shooter in Broncos' history as well as ending up third on both the Santa Clara all-time scoring (1,689 points) and steals (147) charts.

"To coach Steve has been probably the ultimate for a coach, at least from my point of view," said Dick Davey. "He's the epitome of what a coach wants. He makes the game so much easier for me because he can dictate what we do out there with intelligence and skill. And so, from that standpoint, we've had a premier, unbelievable player in our program. Hopefully someday we'll have another chance to have somebody like him.

"What Steve graduating will do for me is probably make me want to go on sabbatical next year and let somebody else coach the team," Davey added with a chuckle. "It's going to be a tremendous loss. And I feel that way, obviously, about all of our seniors — we have five of them — but Steve is a unique player and he brought a unique package to Santa Clara. I'm sure he would have to any team in the country. We're going to really miss him."

On the day his college career came to a close, Steve Nash could see past the immediate loss.

"I would have loved to have gone to a Final Four or a Sweet Sixteen, for that matter," he said. "But not everyone can do that. I had a great time and I got a tremendous amount out of it.

"I can only look at it as how fortunate I am to go through all of this. I tried my best from day one and there will be a tomorrow."

For Steve Nash, there most certainly would be.

In his four years at Santa Clara University, Steve Nash definitely left his mark on the Broncos' record book and in the hearts of Broncos' fans and boosters. According to Dick Davey, coaching a player like Steve was "the ultimate."

Chapter Eight

THE POST - SEASON

He was airborne, 30,000 feet, winging his way toward the most exciting moment of his life. But all Steve Nash could think about as he leaned back against his seat in the Air Canada Airbus was how he wished he was anywhere but on another airplane.

In the six-week period leading up to the 1996 NBA draft, Steve had been inside one too many aircraft. He had visited nine NBA clubs for private workouts and personal evaluations as well as attending both the Nike Desert Classic in Phoenix and the NBA's mandatory pre-draft evaluation camp in Chicago.

It had been six weeks of hotel rooms, taxis, airports and gymnasiums, all combined with writing final exams and graduating from Santa Clara University. It all seemed like a bizarre blur to Steve now and, mercifully, it was finally over. Well, almost over.

As Steve shut his eyes during this four-and-a-half hour flight from Vancouver to Montreal, the second leg in a Victoria-to-New Jersey, all-day air marathon, he knew he still had one workout remaining. He would audition for the Knicks the next day in Westchester, New York, before heading back for the draft in East Rutherford, New Jersey.

It was hard to believe but the National Basketball Association draft, the moment he had been building toward for so many years, was now just four days away.

The Knicks' visit would bring the number of clubs for whom Steve had worked out privately to ten, representing more than a third of the NBA's 29-team membership. It had been a draining process in which Steve had travelled to Portland, Vancouver, Denver, Sacramento, Minneapolis, Indiana, Boston, Phoenix and Charlotte.

During that time, he had been poked, prodded and questioned. He had also discovered what it was like to be viewed as a commodity, as a potential asset of a multi-million dollar sports corporation. It had been an eye-opening, sometimes exciting, experience but now Steve just wanted to get it all over with. He wanted to be drafted.

The post-season had been quite a whirlwind for Steve Nash even before the individual team evaluations got underway.

Just two weeks after Santa Clara's exit from the NCAA Tournament in mid March, Steve had been flown to New York City for the NCAA's annual three-point shooting and slam dunk competition at Fordham University.

The event was held in conjunction with the 1996 NCAA Final Four, which was being staged in East Rutherford on the same weekend. And the honour of being invited to showcase his long-range shooting ability on national television had certainly helped take some of the sting off the fact that Steve's college basketball career was over.

Despite his reputation as a deadly outside shooter, Steve had never before entered a three-point competition, a curious exercise in which shooters are required to pull balls off stationary racks and throw up five shots from each of five designated spots on the floor, all within a one-minute time limit.

Ever the competitor, Steve hadn't been content simply to take part in this event. To get a bit of an edge, he and his visiting California agent, Bill

Duffy, had hit Victoria's Oak Bay high school gym for a quick practice session just before Steve left home to compete in the made-for-TV event.

The practice had obviously paid off, as Steve went on to dominate the three-point competition, beating Oklahoma forward Ryan Minor 18-12 during the championship final in the packed Fordham gym. In the semifinal, Steve amassed an event-record 22 points (out of a possible 30) during an impressive victory over Duke guard Chris Collins.

As Steve proceeded to drain his first seven shots en route to crushing Minor in the three-point final, excitable ESPN announcer Dick Vitale was himself in high gear, gushing over Nash, referring to him as "The Canadian Comet!"

"It's over, baby!" Vitale extolled as Steve sunk three after three. "This is an M&Mer! It's a mismatch. That trophy is going back to Santa Clara and up to Canada!"

"He'll have a tough time getting that through customs," quipped fellow ESPN announcer John Saunders, himself a Canadian.

In the Fordham stands, Dick Davey was justifiably proud and happy to see Steve Nash showing basketball fans across the country what a terrific shooter he was. "What was running through my mind," Davey would say later, "was how well he has represented Santa Clara. He really continues to put our name on the map."

Meanwhile, Steve was grinning ear to ear in the post-competition interviews. This trip had been a lot of fun and to win in such impressive fashion was a huge bonus.

"I was due," Steve told the Associated Press, in a reference to his poor shooting day against

Kansas just a couple of weeks earlier at Tempe. "I had a great time today, a fun ride. What better way to end my college career."

While the national three-point competition had been fun and certainly hadn't hurt his reputation any, the serious post-season evaluation process for Steve Nash would actually begin at the Nike Desert Classic in Phoenix a couple of weeks later.

This post-season appearance would be as important for Steve Nash as any of the 37 other NBA hopefuls who had been invited to the week-long camp. Despite four standout years at Santa Clara, there still seemed to be serious questions about Steve's quickness and athletic ability.

Sometimes it seemed as if those questions were based as much on racial stereotypes as anything else. There seemed to be a popular perception that a player wasn't an "athlete" if he happened to be white.

"I think a lot of people lose sight of what an athlete is and I think that too much emphasis is put on running and jumping," Steve said. "And besides, I don't think I'm as bad as some people think, quickness-wise or jumping-wise."

"I'm not worried about racial stereotyping," he added. "I think that NBA players are more educated than other people. They know that white guys can play — if you're in the league, unless you're a big stiff twelfth man, NBA players know you can play. The colour of skin isn't important to the players. They've been out there and had John Stockton go for 20 assists on them. They've been out there and had Jeff Hornacek

light them up. They know that white guys can play."

Regardless of their basis, the nagging questions about Steve's quickness and athletic ability lingered in the weeks before the Desert Classic. And those questions were summed up in a *Globe and Mail* column by Neil A. Campbell, who quoted an anonymous NBA scout as his main source.

"Your man Steve Nash, he's taken as big a fall as anybody in the draft," the scout had told Campbell. "Right now, he's maybe at the tail end of the first round, beginning of the second round."

Campbell also wrote that NBA scouts were generally disappointed by how Steve had responded to pressure surrounding him during his senior year with the Broncos. "It highlighted his lack of overall speed and quickness," the anonymous scout said. "He'd be in the bottom half of the [NBA] on the quickness scale."

Campbell went on to speculate that Steve could conceivably still be around for the Vancouver Grizzlies who, besides having a high lottery pick, were also scheduled to open the second round of the NBA draft with the number 30 pick overall.

Another journalist who regularly covered the Grizzlies offered a particularly harsh opinion of Steve's NBA prospects. During an open-phones segment on Vancouver CFMI's Sportstalk radio show, Gary Kingston of the Vancouver *Sun* suggested that if fans really wanted to see Steve Nash play pro hoops, they could save some money by waiting just a year until he was out of the NBA and then driving down to Yakima, Washington to watch him play in the Continental Basketball Association.

Indeed, predictions for where Steve would go in the draft or what kind of a career he could expect in the NBA were all over the map. The Oakland *Tribune*, after consulting with scouts and management types, rated Steve anywhere from number 14 in the first round to an early second-rounder. As the Phoenix camp approached, Steve was still considered by most to be a first-rounder, but that was by no means a sure thing.

The opinions that Steve valued most were those of the NBA players who were familiar with his game, players such as Jason Kidd of the Dallas Mavericks and Gary Payton of the Seattle Sonics, a pair of all-stars with whom Steve had worked out during the previous summer.

"I compare him to John Stockton," Kidd told the San Jose *Mercury News* in one article.

"Right now, he's got a lot of Mark Price in him. Jeff Hornacek, too," Payton said in the same story.

But Payton had attached a rider, describing Steve as a "work in progress" who would have to develop defensively or risk being embarrassed in the NBA.

"If he had to guard someone one-on-one, he wouldn't do so well right now," Payton had observed to the *Mercury News*. "On a team like ours [Seattle], he has to play defence or he'll sit down. Here [in the NBA], guards will not let him shoot at free range. He has to adjust to what comes at him."

Steve had taken the constructive criticism as exactly that. "I think it's the same with anybody who comes into the league," he said. "I don't see too many guys who don't get hurt defensively in their rookie year. I think everybody gets taken to school a few times at least."

Steve's draft status seemed to hinge on two things. The first factor would be his performance in post-season camps and team visits. The second would be which college underclassmen decided to declare themselves eligible for the NBA draft. If Georgetown University sophomore Allen Iverson and Georgia Tech freshman Stephon Marbury stayed in school, Steve could conceivably be the first point guard chosen on June 26th in New Jersey. If those players came out, he could drop in the draft no matter how well he performed during the post-season.

"I think Steve Nash can definitely play," offered Toronto Raptors' NBA rookie of the year Damon Stoudamire. "The messed up thing about the college game is that so many underclassmen come out in the draft. I think how high Steve goes will probably be contingent on how many underclassmen come out. But I think Steve is definitely a player who can play at this level. I watched him play and I played against him for three straight years. He's definitely a ballplayer."

Portland assistant general manager and former NBA player Jim Paxson agreed. He compared Nash to his younger brother, John, a longtime backcourt mate of Michael Jordan with the Chicago Bulls who carved out a fine NBA career without being exceptionally quick or an outstanding leaper.

"Steve could be the first point guard chosen in the draft if those guys [Iverson and Marbury] don't come out," Paxson observed as the Phoenix camp approached. "We look at Steve as a very solid player. There's a place for Steve Nash in our league. He's a kid with good skills who does everything right."

It often seemed as if the tone of speculation about Nash depended upon how much a scout or a general manager had been exposed to the Santa Clara star. Many of those who had seen him play a lot had seemingly been converted. Those who had but fleeting contact remained skeptical heading into Phoenix.

The man who had seen the most of Steve Nash during his four years at Santa Clara, the man who had been through it all with this Canadian point guard, had no reservations about his future as a pro.

"There are a lot of doubters out there," Dick Davey told the Seattle *Times*. "But I think he's going to be a tremendous pro or I'm not very smart. Someone is going to be very lucky."

The Nike Desert Classic is an annual showcase of some of the best senior talent in the NCAA. It is a week-long invitational tournament run by the NBA and the Phoenix Suns at America West Arena in downtown Phoenix. The top few prospects in the draft often skip this event, but the talent level remains high from year to year.

The 38 players invited to the Desert Classic are divided into four teams, which then go head-to-head for the benefit of pro scouts and management. It is a chance for NBA people to see some of the top graduating college players against similarly talented opposition and playing under NBA coaches, strategies and rules.

After Steve's roller-coaster senior season with the Broncos, most scouts believed Phoenix was the key to his draft status. A good camp could solidify his position as a mid-to-late first-rounder, perhaps even move him up in the draft. A bad week in the desert could conceivably move Steve off the first-round board altogether.

The prevailing feeling seemed to be that Steve needed to prove he could do the same things against some of the NCAA's best players that he had done so routinely against the perceived weaker competition of the West Coast Conference. The scouts were eager to see how well he was able to keep the country's quicker guards in front of him on defence and whether he could get by top players on the dribble.

The looming question seemed to be whether Steve was quick enough to be a starting guard in the NBA. And unless he had at least the potential to be a starter, teams would be unlikely to risk a relatively high first-round pick on him.

Those who had been around him most had no doubts. "Whoever gets Steve is going to be shocked at how good he is," Santa Clara coach Dick Davey predicted in the Oakland *Tribune*. "He's hurting a bit right now. He wasn't hurt the last three years and was able to go by everybody."

Unfortunately, as Steve entered this crucial Phoenix camp, he was still on the limp, the hamstring problem which had plagued him during the loss to Kansas still nagging at him daily, hampering his every movement. For a few days, Steve and agent Bill Duffy had debated whether he should attend the Desert Classic at all. They knew Steve was taking a tremendous risk by showing up in Phoenix at less than full strength. But they were also tired of people doubting his ability. Steve just wanted to show everybody, once and for all, that he could play the game.

Steve Nash brings the ball up the floor under watchful eyes of NBA scouts during the Nike Desert Classic at Phoenix, Arizona.

"This is probably the most pressure anybody can have. You play basketball your whole life, you work as hard as you can every day and it all comes down to one week of performance," he conceded before leaving for Phoenix. "If you have one bad week or game, all your hopes and dreams could go down the drain. You've got to be ready."

The injury meant Steve wasn't nearly as ready as he would have liked. But he felt going to the Desert Classic was the right move to make.

"I just want to go play," he said. "I can possibly help myself there."

The gamble would pay off as Steve erased virtually all major doubts about his abilities. Despite his lingering hamstring injury, he proved he was a far better defensive player than many had given him credit for. And with a lineup of talented teammates that included Kentucky's Final Four MVP Tony Delk and Donta Bright of the University of Massachusetts, scouts finally saw what Steve was capable of doing when the talent level around him was comparable.

During his three Desert Classic games in America West Arena, Steve averaged eight assists, seven points and nearly four steals while sharing time at the point on his team with Moochie Norris, a senior from West Florida. More importantly, Steve proved without a doubt to NBA observers that he could run a team. He had legitimized himself as a solid first-round pick.

"I was astounded how good Nash was in Phoenix," Vancouver Grizzlies assistant coach Rex Hughes would later tell *Sports Only* magazine. "I thought he was a tremendous player. He does everything you have to do to play in a point guard position in this league."

"Watching him in that environment in Phoenix, he was totally in charge of his team," added Ken Shields, who was in Arizona to catch part of the Desert Classic. "Steve was the dominant player on the floor, running the operation with his team. When he spoke, everybody listened. He rallied the team, got them together at the right times. Plus, his technical ability on the floor to make

NBA director of scouting Marty Blake and Steve Nash. Blake had this to say about Steve : "He's a point guard. They are born."

the right decision and then get the ball to the right person with the correct pass at the right time was special."

Steve's performance in America West answered some nagging questions about his quickness and his defensive ability. It also earned him a spot on the Desert Classic's five-man tournament all-star team. Steve had definitely opened some eyes.

It wasn't just NBA scouts who had noticed, either. In a restaurant, while Steve was chatting with some people from the Celtics organization, he noticed NBA legend Larry Bird sitting at the Boston table. Bird looked up and nodded: "Mr. Nash," he said quietly.

To be recognized by one of the greatest players in NBA history was a huge thrill for Steve, as was another instance after his first game of the Desert Classic when then Phoenix Suns' superstar Charles Barkley greeted him as he walked by. "Hey, you're a good player," Sir Charles said to Steve. "Keep working hard."

While Steve was working on the court at Phoenix, Bill Duffy was busy working the sidelines and the back rooms for the benefit of his new client. Steve had known Duffy, a former Santa Clara player himself, since his sophomore year with the Broncos. And by December of his senior year,

Steve had already pretty much decided that Duffy would eventually be his agent.

This was a dicey issue, however, since NCAA rules prohibit an athlete from actually hiring an agent until after his eligibility expires. But although no formal agreement was in place, Steve had made the fact he was leaning toward signing with Duffy and his SportsWest Management Group of Alamo, California perfectly clear to the 30 other agencies that had made early inquiries through his parents in Victoria.

Duffy, who along with partner Aaron Goodwin also works with NBA veterans such as Jason Kidd, Gary Payton, Antonio Davis and Terrell Brandon, spent the week in Phoenix talking to general managers and scouts of NBA clubs, trying to get a feel for where Steve was going to go in the draft. And after Steve's performance in the Desert Classic, it had become clear to Duffy that there was a great deal of interest.

The individual pre-draft ritual for potential first-round picks is an exhaustive evaluation process that is unfamiliar to the average basketball fan. But considering the type of money that is being thrown around by NBA teams for rookies — with first-round picks guaranteed as much as $3 million US a year for three years — it pays for teams to be careful.

General managers want to be as certain as possible on draft day that they aren't adopting an expensive problem child. They have to be knowledgeable about every potential pick who might come their way through the natural order of the draft or as part of some last-minute trade. Since there is a strict five-minute time limit between first-round picks on draft night, each team's information has to be current and reliable.

A typical visit to an NBA team by Steve Nash during the spring of 1996 was a one- or two-day process that included three main components — the workout, the psychological assessment and the interview. Often that interview would come in the form of a meal with a team's general manager or coaching staff.

Some clubs go deeper than others when checking out a player. Some even hire private investigators to check a player's background, character and whether he has a history of drug or alcohol abuse. Ever since the 1986 NBA draft, from which several of the top picks fizzled out because of substance abuse problems, league teams don't leave anything to chance.

Steve's most unusual experience came during his first club visit — on May 13 to Portland. During a two-day session in which he scrimmaged with a collection of nine CBA players and free agents, Steve was also asked to submit to a psychological test. During this test, he was shown an ink pattern on a plain, white page.

"Use your imagination," a Trail Blazers representative had told him, "and tell me what this is."

"It looks like when you're in elementary school and you throw paint on a paper and fold it over and you've got a symmetrical object," Steve replied. He wasn't sure if this test was serious. "Is this a joke?" he thought. "Do they want me to say: 'OK, this is the joke — you got me'; or do they really want me to answer these questions?"

The Portland test didn't really surprise Steve. Somebody else had told him, facetiously, during one of his visits: "We've got to give you this psychological analysis to find out whether you're an axe-murderer or not. But if you make 50 per cent of your threes, we don't care if you're an axe-murderer."

Many clubs have a series of specific physical tests which they run draft prospects through. In Charlotte, Steve surprised Hornets staff by breaking the team's agility drill record. In Indianapolis, he stunned Pacers people by dunking the ball off a one-dribble run.

Some visits were long; Steve spent the better part of two days in Portland and three in Minnesota. Others were brief; he was in and out of Boston before he knew it.

In a late visit to the Phoenix Suns, Steve shot around for just 20 minutes before his hamstring began to tighten up. Suns assistant coach Danny Ainge told him not to worry about doing anything else. "I've seen you play. I know what you can do," Ainge told Steve. "I hope you'll be around when we pick."

Mostly these workouts and meetings were just a last-minute reassurance for NBA clubs, whose scouting staffs had already spent much of the previous winter determining whether each of these prospects was capable of playing in the NBA. This was a chance for general managers and coaches to meet players and spend a little time with them. Attitude and character would be taken into account as well as physical ability.

Medical testing came during the league's official pre-draft camp over the first weekend of June in Chicago. This annual camp is mandatory for all players entering the draft, including underclassmen, although few of the top picks actually play any basketball there, instead opting to simply submit to the compulsory medical testing the league requires.

The Chicago testing lasted four days and was by far the most extensive physical examination Steve had ever undergone. Each draftee submitted to four hours a day of tests to determine his general health as well as his basketball-specific statistics and capacities such as height, weight, leaping ability, hand-eye co-ordination and peripheral vision. Many of the tests were electronic and they reminded Steve of playing in a video arcade.

On most of his NBA visits, Steve Nash would slip in and out of town inconspicuously, doing an interview or two with the teams' beat writers or local television. But his visit to Vancouver in mid-May attracted more attention than usual.

The Vancouver Grizzlies had been linked to Steve virtually since their admission to the NBA and many Vancouver fans wondered if the Grizzlies would somehow find a way to draft this rare homegrown hoops hero.

Realistically, the Grizzlies were not in the right position to draft Steve Nash. With the number three pick overall in the draft, they were too high to justifiably select him. And it was now highly unlikely the Victoria point guard would slip far enough for the Grizzlies to obtain him with the first pick in the second round.

Grizzlies president and general manager Stu

Jackson described the addition of Nash to his lineup as a "no-brainer" from a marketing standpoint. But the Grizzlies had also been careful about their public assessment of Nash's abilities. They knew they weren't likely to draft in Steve's range and they didn't want to raise public expectations about the chances of landing him.

And so Steve's visit to the Grizzlies, which came in conjunction with a celebrity golf tournament he had been invited to play in Vancouver, was treated by the British Columbia sports media as a public relations exercise. The Grizzlies, it was speculated, had to at least bring in Steve for a workout, but there was little chance he would end up with Vancouver on draft day.

Trades to move up and down in the draft are always a possibility, ever-careful Jackson told the Vancouver *Sun*, adding that the Grizzlies needed to "cover any eventuality" with such a visit.

Steve dined with Jackson at a chic Vancouver restaurant to open his visit and then had breakfast the next morning with Grizzlies coaches Brian Winters and Rex Hughes. Then it was time for a two-hour workout at the Grizzlies' training facility in suburban Richmond.

Nash's appearance at the Grizzlies' gym still drew considerable attention from the local media, who were allowed in to watch the final few minutes of his workout. On his final free-throw, he banked in the ball off the glass and then

When Steve Nash visited the Vancouver Grizzlies for a pre-draft workout and evaluation, he displayed his basketball skills for Grizzlies staff, spoke with members of the media, and was tested and measured for strength, wingspan, height, weight and vertical reach. Steve underwent similar visits to ten different NBA clubs in the six weeks leading up to the draft.

winked at the journalists who had gathered to speak with him. In several interviews with the Vancouver media, Steve described the opportunity to work out for the expansion Grizzlies as "a dream come true."

"Regardless of what I do the rest of my life, I can tell my kids I worked out for the Grizzlies," Steve told the *Sun*.

Inside, Steve still held some hope that the Grizzlies could work something out to land him on draft day. Although the pundits suggested there would be too much pressure playing as the NBA's lone true Canadian product in his home province, being close to family and friends was still Steve's first choice.

"I tried to come in here and shoot the lights out so I could put some heat on these guys, try to make them make a move, but unless they make a move, they're not going to take me. I'm not going to be in the top three or four picks," Steve told the *Sun* after working out for the Grizzlies.

The Grizzlies would eventually swing a deal in an apparent attempt to land Steve Nash. In a trade with the Houston Rockets just a week prior to the draft, they obtained the number 22 pick in the first round. They would cross their fingers that Nash would still be available at that spot while at the same time exploring the possibility of using that pick in a trade to move up a few more spots.

As draft day drew closer, however, it was apparent that Steve would go higher than the Grizzlies' number 22 spot. *Sport* Magazine rated him twentieth but some speculation had him going as high as number five overall to Minnesota, a team hungry for a point guard. Most other publications and prognosticators had him going somewhere in between.

The Don Leventhal NBA Draft Report, a document that annually ranks the top 200 college prospects and is considered an authority of pre-draft analysis, rated Steve at number 17 overall. It also ranked him as the third best point guard prospect in the draft behind Allen Iverson and Stephon Marbury, who by this time had both declared themselves eligible among a record 36 underclassmen making it the youngest draft in NBA history.

The Leventhal Report also seemed to sum up what most scouts were thinking about Steve's up-and-down senior season at Santa Clara.

"He probably put too much pressure on himself and tried to do too much as he persevered through a season in which he knew that loads of NBA scouts were at every one of his games and were watching his every step," Leventhal's report said. "I have a strong feeling that once he makes it to the NBA, gets confident with his new team and settles in, he will eventually develop into one of the league's top playmakers and long-range shooters."

The fact that Steve's stock had risen since the end of the NCAA season was also reflected in comments made by Timberwolves coach Flip Saunders after Nash's visit to Minneapolis at the end of May.

"He is a lot like [Utah star John] Stockton," Saunders told the Minneapolis *Star Tribune*. "What they lack in athletic ability, they make up in other things. He's probably more mature and ready to play in the NBA [than Iverson or Marbury]. Nash is a guy who can be in this league a long time."

The speculation about where and how high Steve would go would continue to mount right up until draft day. Almost daily, a new report or rumour had one club or another apparently interested in picking him. And at least once daily, somebody would ask him The Question: "So, where are you going to go?"

Ironically, Steve had about as much idea as the average fan. All of his workouts had gone at least reasonably well and he had received an especially good feeling from a few clubs — Minnesota, Indiana, Charlotte and Portland among them. But his draft status was still a guess at best.

Much of the pre-draft talk regarding Steve had centered on the Minnesota Timberwolves, the Indiana Pacers and the Charlotte Hornets. The T-Wolves, desperate for a point guard, had put Steve up for three days in Minneapolis. Minnesota picked at number five, higher than Steve was rated, but VP Kevin McHale was believed to be trying to swing a deal to move up, for Georgia Tech's Stephon Marbury, or down, to pick Steve. Still, there was some speculation by NBA writers that the T-Wolves might even pick Steve fifth.

The most popular pre-draft prediction had Steve going number ten overall to the Indiana Pacers, although the Pacers seemed to already have their point guard of the future in Travis Best. *Sports Illustrated* picked Steve at number ten, to Indiana, as did the Los Angeles *Times*, Vancouver *Sun* and Vancouver *Province*. Several other predictions, including one by *USA Today*, had

Steve going to the Charlotte Hornets, who held both the thirteenth and sixteenth picks in the first round, while New Jersey's *The Record* had Steve going fifteenth to Phoenix.

Steve heard and read all the rumours just like any other NBA fan. All he could do was hope that through the workouts and post-draft camps he had impressed enough people to ensure that he would be a first-rounder, perhaps even a high first-rounder.

That first-round status was essential. It would mean a guaranteed three-year contract and an NBA pension. It would also mean a minimum of half a million dollars per year for playing the game he loved.

Slipping into the second round would bring uncertainty — less money and no job security. Such a slip was highly unlikely at this point, but Steve knew that nothing was guaranteed.

Still, he wasn't spending these final days obsessing about his draft prospects. Steve felt he had done his work. Now it was out of his hands.

Besides, there wasn't much time these days to dwell on anything. As the draft approached, Steve became one of the hottest stories in Canadian sport. And in the few days before he had departed for the New York area with his family, the attention had reached ridiculous proportions.

Steve was still completing team visits and working at Jason Kidd's basketball camp in Dallas in the week before the draft. He had decided to return to Victoria for one day, a day on which he hoped to kick back with family and friends. But this day would turn out to be far from relaxing.

Steve was barely out of bed and had yet to pour a bowl of cereal when the first reporter showed up at his parents' home. Minutes later, the house was invaded by a television crew from "Inside Stuff", the NBA's slick, in-house magazine show.

CBC called. Could they send a crew over? The *Financial Post* wanted to do an interview and a photo shoot. A Las Vegas sports radio station phoned. So did BCTV, TSN, a Vancouver sports talk radio show and a number of U.S. and Canadian newspapers. During one brief telephone conversation, Steve had seven call-waiting beeps. It was driving him crazy.

When would draft day finally arrive?

Less than one week before the draft, Steve Nash shoots hoops on the school court behind his parents' Victoria home for the benefit of a camera crew from the NBA's "Inside Stuff".

On second thought, as Steve and his family winged their way from Montreal to New Jersey on this Saturday before the NBA draft, maybe an airplane wasn't such a bad place to be. At least it was private and the telephone wasn't ringing.

As their plane descended from the cloud cover, the vast and jagged New York area skyline quickly spread out beneath them. A few minutes later, they landed at Newark airport. Out of the cabin window, the Nashes could see the team plane bearing the logo and colours of the Phoenix Suns.

Suddenly, the realization hit Steve. All those years of dribbling and shooting on the playground and in the gym were about to pay off.

It was no longer a dream. He was finally here. Suddenly it was real.

Chapter Nine

D - DAY IN NEW JERSEY

For millions of New Yorkers, it was just a typical summer afternoon, about 85 degrees and humid, with the stench of garbage occasionally flaring the nostrils. And, of course, there was the traffic, with hundreds of cars inching through the Lincoln Tunnel connecting the towering Manhattan high-rises to the freeways and swampland of New Jersey.

Steve Nash was beginning to get anxious as the car he was riding in crawled through the afternoon traffic jam. This was certainly not a typical day for the 22-year-old from Victoria. This was the day he had been dreaming about since the eighth grade, the day he would officially join the National Basketball Association.

Steve had spent the morning with Metropolitan Sports Enterprises, a Manhattan sports modeling firm that had courted him since his arrival in New York. The agency had outfitted him with $3,000 worth of new clothes from Perry Ellis, hired a fashion photographer to feature him in a sports-wear portfolio and hosted Steve and his friends at exclusive Manhattan clubs and restaurants. For a college kid accustomed to hanging around in jeans and basketball shorts, this exposure to the world of high fashion had certainly been different.

The modeling opportunity was just one of many doors Steve's newfound status was opening for him. The past few days had been a kick, but now he was getting nervous. He just wanted to get back to his New Jersey hotel in time to get dressed and get drafted.

It was really the first time all week that Steve had felt anxious. He had enjoyed draft week immensely, sharing the parties and the excellent meals staged by the NBA with his visiting friends and family.

Gathered in New Jersey to celebrate the draft with Steve was a contingent of about 25, ranging from relatives and family friends to former teammates from Santa Clara, high school and even junior high.

The trip had begun with two nights for the immediate Nash family on the 36th floor of Manhattan's Dumont Plaza Hotel, a fringe benefit while Steve completed his final pre-draft workout with the Knicks as well as a speaking engagement at a Knicks' youth basketball camp. As Steve took care of business, Jean, John and Joann played tourist, shopping Fifth Avenue and riding to the top of the Empire State Building. And as luck would have it, they were able to combine this sightseeing with an opportunity to watch the soccer game of younger brother Martin, who was in New York for a contest with the American Professional Soccer League's Vancouver 86ers.

Even after moving across to New Jersey, the site of the draft, the Nashes had continued to enjoy a nice taste of Manhattan. The NBA had treated the invited draftees' families to the Broadway musical "Smoky Joe's Cafe", where Joann spotted Patrick Swayze, and to a late-night outing at the All-Star Cafe, where the Nashes saw Patrick Ewing, Gregory Hines and Spike Lee, among other celebrities. And Steve had found time each night to slip away from New Jersey back to Manhattan to party with his visiting friends and his cousin Lee, who had flown all the way from London, England for the draft.

There were also some responsibilities to take care of during draft week, however. Besides his involvement with the modeling agency and several mandatory player meetings called by the NBA, Steve was also expected to accommodate the media.

The major pre-draft interview session had come on the eve of draft day at the Sheraton Meadowlands. Each of nine pre-selected players was slotted in for a half-hour, during which time Steve sat at his own designated table in one of the hotel's large ballrooms. When his session began, Steve's table had been virtually empty while the tables of fellow point guards Allen Iverson and Stephon Marbury had been virtually swallowed up by reporters. But eventually, Steve was also surrounded by print, radio and television reporters and the air around his table hummed with the whir of camera motordrives.

Despite the fact he had proven himself again and again throughout his college career and during the post-draft evaluation period, Steve was still being widely portrayed as an underdog. "Steve Nash has sort of gotten lost in the shuffle among point guards in the NBA draft," *USA Today* would write.

"They're tremendous players. They deserve a lot of attention," Steve had said, alluding to the incredible attention Iverson and Marbury were receiving before the draft. "They've been on the scene for many years. You know, Stephon probably got more attention in high school than I did in my four years at college. But that's what happens when you're a New York City legend. I don't resent that fact. Not everybody can have the same path."

Besides the recognition questions, Steve had also dealt over and over again with the Canadian angle to his story. How did such a basketball talent ever emerge from a hockey-playing nation?

Did he feel he was carrying the hopes of an entire country into the draft? What did he think of his chances of being picked by Vancouver?

"I'm not going to concern myself with speculating about what's going to happen and what moves are going to be made," he told reporter after reporter. "So many things could happen that it's really impossible to tell.

"Going to Vancouver is a situation where it's a long shot, so we're just going to have to see what happens. Right now, I'm enjoying every minute of this week. It's only going to happen to me once."

Certainly, he had enjoyed himself during the past four days. But now, as Steve sat in this car, crawling from Manhattan to New Jersey, the reason for all of this hype, all this celebration, was drawing closer. Enjoyment had given way to anxiety. How long was this trip going to take?

Steve felt relieved as the car eventually exited the tunnel and began to weave its way toward East Rutherford. When he finally spotted the 21-story tower of the Sheraton Meadowlands, he knew everything would be all right. At least he wouldn't be sitting in traffic when his name was called.

Steve arrived back at the 19th-floor room he was sharing with his cousin Lee to find a crowd of his buddies watching the European Cup soccer semifinal showdown between England and Germany on television. Most of the room was rooting for England with the exception of Santa Clara teammate Phil Von Buchwaldt, a native of France, and Ron Schubert, a family friend from Vancouver with German roots. Watching this game with a bunch of guys he felt close to was a great way to wipe away the draft-day nerves. As Steve sat there cheering on England in its eventual shoot-out loss, he felt comfortable again.

A couple of hours later, Steve was freshly showered and dressed in the stylish, loose-fitting black suit that had been custom made for him by an Atlanta tailor who traditionally outfits NBA players. He then rode the elevator down the to the lobby to catch the players' shuttle to the Continental Airlines Arena where the draft would be held.

The shuttle was scheduled to leave the hotel at 5:45 p.m. But it was 6:15 by the time it left after widely-predicted overall number one pick Allen Iverson showed up late. Another highly-rated draftee, Cal forward Shareef Abdur-Rahim, missed the bus altogether and would eventually catch up with the rest of the players later.

As the shuttle pulled out of the parking lot, each player on board was headed toward one of the defining moments of his young life. The draftees broke the tension by talking and joking amongst themselves during the five-minute ride to the arena. Everybody on this bus had a common bond that would last their entire careers. They also had each other's respect.

"You nervous?" Steve asked, nodding toward Iverson, the fellow point guard from Georgetown whom everybody expected to go first overall.

"No," Iverson replied. "No reason to be nervous now. Come this far."

As the bus pulled up to the huge, white arena, the players could see fans milling around the building, wearing the jerseys of their favourite college or NBA teams pulled over t-shirts. Hundreds of fans crowded around souvenir booths and the temporary hoops that had been set up in the parking lot for pre-draft shooting contests. These fans would each dish out $15 to enter an arena on a beautiful summer evening, not to actually watch a basketball game but just to see where their college heroes would be starting their pro careers.

Once inside the arena, the 1996 draftees posed for a group photo with NBA commissioner David Stern. They were then sequestered in the Green Room, a private area located behind the monolithic 50-foot high draft stage that had been assembled in one end of the arena.

A half-hour later, the Green Room began to fill up as the nine special guests of each invited draftee arrived on separate shuttles. Joining Steve at one of the round banquet tables assigned to each player were his immediate family, his friend Mandesa Milton from Portland, his aunt Janice and cousin Lee from England, his agent Bill Duffy, and Nancy Miller, the mother of Jamie Miller, Steve's old high school buddy from Victoria.

Steve was thrilled that his family could be right here with him to share in this evening. It had all started out as his own wide-eyed dream way back in junior high but it belonged to the whole Nash household now.

A half-hour before the draft was scheduled to begin, the Nash family snuck out of the Green Room for a peek at the arena set-up. They stood along the back of the media area, staring up at the gigantic draft stage that bore the colourful logos of the NBA teams beside the number where each would pick in the first round. In the next couple of hours, their Steve would be wearing one of those logos. It was really happening.

The Green Room on draft night is a room full of hope and tension. Only a maximum of 20 players are invited to the draft as guests of the NBA, and the league tries to be certain that all 20 will indeed go in the first round so that nobody ends up embarrassed. Still, it isn't easy for any draft hopeful to sit there, as team after team makes its pick, not knowing for sure where, when — or even if — his name will be called.

Making it even stranger for the players is that they are hidden away backstage while the draft is actually taking place. As Steve Nash sat at the table with his family on his special night, watching the proceedings on a TV monitor, he felt strangely as though he wasn't really at the draft at all.

Steve had heard about so many potential scenarios regarding his draft status that he didn't know what to expect. He knew he would not be among the top four picks, so he was able to relax somewhat as Allen Iverson went number one overall, as expected, to the Philadelphia 76ers.

But after Stephon Marbury had gone to the Milwaukee Bucks at number four, Steve knew that anything was now within the realm of possibility. Minnesota, which was to pick at number five, needed a point guard and Steve had heard rumours that there was a chance he could even be selected that high by the Timberwolves.

That bubble burst five minutes later, however, when Minnesota selected Connecticut shooting guard Ray Allen, who would later be shipped off to Milwaukee in a draft-floor trade which secured Marbury for the Timberwolves. Then Steve watched another scenario pass by as Indiana, which had been widely rumoured to be picking him at number ten, opted instead for centre Erick Dampier of Mississippi State.

Jean Nash fretted as she sat at her son's table, waiting, promising her good friend Nancy Miller that she wouldn't cry. Her heart was racing. She didn't care where Steve ended up or how much money he made. She just couldn't stand the thought of her son being disappointed on the night for which he had worked so hard and so long. John Nash felt the same way. "The worst thing is if you sit in that room and you sit and you sit and you sit and he doesn't get picked," he said as the pre-draft tension built. "The longer it goes, the worse you feel for him."

Three picks later, Steve's heart was pounding again when it was Charlotte's turn to select at number 13. But the Hornets chose Pennsylvania high school star Kobe Bryant, a 17-year-old guard. Sacramento, well-stocked at the point, then selected Greek league forward Predrag Stojakovic at number 14.

Steve wasn't worried. It was nearly one-and-a-half hours into the draft, but he knew that, somewhere during the next four picks, he would be taken. Phoenix, Charlotte, Portland and New York were up next, in that order. One of those teams would snap him up.

The Phoenix Suns had the next pick. And even before David Stern stepped up to the microphone to announce their selection, Steve knew this was it. Just as Stern began to make his way toward the stage, the TNT cameraman stationed in the Green Room scurried over to the Nash table. A couple of seconds later, Steve watched on TV as Stern said the magic words he had been imagining for nearly ten years. "With the 15th pick in the 1996 NBA draft, the Phoenix Suns select Steve Nash of the University of Santa Clara."

Steve rose from his seat and immediately found his mother. He wrapped Jean Nash in a huge, warm hug. "You're a wonderful Mom and you've helped me so much," he began.

Martin Nash jumped up to embrace his older brother. In the confusion, Jean was bumped back into the chair behind her. She would have fallen over completely had Nancy Miller not broken her fall. In the confusion, Jean Nash didn't even see the TV screen as her son ascended the podium.

Steve's Aunt Janice, who had came all the way from London, England for the draft, had been a little confused by the events leading up to his selection. "What does this mean?" she asked everybody at the table as each pick was made. When her nephew's name was called at number 15, Janice said: "He does have a job now, right?"

Steve most certainly had a job, but Auntie Janice wasn't sure exactly where. "Where's Phoenix? Is it by Indiana?" she asked. "Oh, it's in the desert," she said, her eyes opening wider. "It's by Las Vegas, then!"

Phoenix could have been on the moon as far as Steve Nash was concerned. All that mattered was that it was in the NBA. He was in the NBA! As Steve turned the corner from the Green Room and stepped into the noisy, packed arena, he was taken aback: "Whoa, there are a lot of people in here," he thought.

Already wearing a white Phoenix Suns baseball cap that had been handed to him by NBA personnel, Steve seemed to be walking in space as he made his way up the short staircase toward the podium and David Stern. He was taking long, slow, exaggerated steps and his face was illuminated in a megawatt smile, each of his eyebrows arched into a peak above an eye filled with absolute wonder. It was a look of pure, unbridled joy.

Steve had never felt so exhilarated. He was walking slowly toward the podium because he was trying to pick out his friends among the crowd of 15,000 in the arena. And there they were. Almost directly in line with commissioner Stern's head, he saw them — Drew Zurek, Kevin Dunne, Jason Sedlock and Phil Von Buchwaldt from his Santa Clara team; Al Whitley, Adam Miller, John Clancy, Chris Isherwood, Brent McLay and Jamie Miller from back home. They were yipping and screaming and raising their arms in the air, clearly enjoying this moment almost as much as Steve.

For an instant, Steve looked right through David Stern, the man whose handshake would officially welcome him into one of the most exclusive clubs in the world. "Wow, you've got a rowdy group of followers," the NBA commissioner smiled.

"Yeah," Steve said, proudly, "they came all the way from Canada."

As he prepared to join the TNT interview crew, one of an endless string of media sessions each draftee had to undergo, Steve raised his fists in the air and pumped them to his friends in the crowd. For a split second everything stopped. There would be no more waiting, no more workouts, no more sitting in the Green Room. It was all over. He had done it.

Steve had known for months that this moment was coming. But now it was sweet validation. It marked the conclusion of a remarkable journey. Less than five years before this moment, he had been suspended because of a school transfer, and was sitting out his grade 11 season. Now here he was, in the NBA. While Stephon Marbury and Allen Iverson talked about their struggles to rise from adversity, Steve thought about his own rise from obscurity. The Canadian kid who four years earlier had practically been forced to beg for a scholarship had just been admitted to the best basketball league in the world.

Steve was shuttled from the immediate live TNT interview to a session on ESPN Radio. Briefly, his friends found him near the side boards of the arena. All eleven reached over the glass, grabbing Steve's shoulders and arms and rocking him back and forth in jubilation before a serious-looking NBA employee with an earphone and a cellular phone whisked their buddy away to a general media scrum.

Of course, the first question any draftee must be asked is: "How does it feel?"

"This is just a dream come true and it's unbelievable," Steve said, wearing a permanent grin during the post-draft press conference as reporters from across North America hunched over his interview table.

A Long Shot pays off: Steve Nash flashes a look of pure and unbridled joy just seconds after hearing his name called as the first-round draft choice of the Phoenix Suns.

Less than an hour after he had officially become a professional basketball player, however, Steve was already learning some lessons about the realities of the business.

The Suns had made him their pick despite the fact they were loaded at the point guard position with former NBA All-Star Kevin Johnson and capable backup Elliot Perry both in the lineup. The trade questions started even before Steve had completely digested the fact that he was going to Phoenix. There was a possibility he could be shipped away in a deal before he even touched a basketball. Jamie Miller, his high school buddy, bought a Suns hat, but kept the sales tag attached, just in case Steve was traded.

"Yeah, I understand that there's a possibility of a trade there, but I'm really not going to get caught up in all that," Steve said as he prepared for live interviews back to Phoenix. "We'll see what happens. This is just a great day for me."

But it wasn't just trade rumours that Steve had to deal with. He soon learned that the Phoenix fans had booed his selection at a draft-night party at America West Arena. The majority of Suns' fans gathered there had wanted Final Four hero John Wallace, a forward from Syracuse University. Wallace's attitude in pre-draft meetings and workouts had caused him to slide from projected mid-lottery status down to number 18, where he eventually went to the New York Knicks. Phoenix fans had been upset when coach Cotton Fitzsimmons announced the selection of Steve rather than Wallace and they had let their feelings be known in rather loud fashion.

After Steve made his way up to the Suns' private box in Continental Airlines Arena, he was hooked up via telephone with members of the Phoenix media. "The fans here booed you. How does it feel?" they asked him.

The fans' reaction had been disappointing for Steve. Certainly, he would have rather been cheered, for the fans to be excited about his acquisition. But he also appreciated the fact that John Wallace carried a far bigger reputation than he did. In one sense, he completely understood the reaction in Phoenix.

"I'm glad that they booed. It showed that they're passionate about their team," Steve said. "I probably would have booed myself, too."

The Suns' brass didn't seem too worried about the fans' reaction. They had been booed in 1988 when they had selected forward Dan Majerle, who turned out to be an NBA All-Star. And they had been booed again in 1995 when they selected forward Michael Finley, who had gone on to make the NBA's all-rookie first team.

"I hope this is three-for-three," Fitzsimmons joked of the fans' reaction to the Nash pick. "I'm not too disappointed with the other two. I think they did fine."

Although there had been some disagreement within the Suns' braintrust on their pick, team president and CEO Jerry Colangelo seemed excited about landing Steve Nash. So did assistant coach Danny Ainge, who had been tabbed to take over from head coach Cotton Fitzsimmons in the near future.

"He is a leader. He can deliver and he can shoot," Jerry Colangelo said of Steve. "This is a very good pick for us. And when you consider the fact that Kevin Johnson is only going to play one more year before he retires, we needed to

Less than half an hour after being drafted, Steve Nash does a radio interview via cellular phone back to his new home town, Phoenix.

start planning in advance and that's what this is all about."

"I think he's a player who will be better in the NBA than he was in college because he's the type of player who makes other guys around him better," Danny Ainge said. "He didn't have that opportunity before [in college]."

Almost lost for Steve in the excitement of draft night were two important factors. The first was that, as the 15th pick, he had become the highest Canadian ever selected in the modern era of the NBA. His selection bettered that of Chicago forward Bill Wennington, who had gone number 16 to the Dallas Mavericks in 1985.

More important, however, was the fact that Steve had become only the second Canadian high school basketball product to be drafted in the first round, joining current CTV analyst and former national team star Leo Rautins, who went 17th overall in 1983 to the Philadelphia 76ers.

That significance was apparently lost on the folks at YTV, Canada's national youth network that had secured the rights to televise the draft live. YTV only dedicated one hour to its coverage and, subsequently, left the draft after the number nine selection. As Steve Nash made Canadian sports history, YTV was airing an episode of "The Flintstones".

Still, the country would see their most high-profile hoops product take the stage later that night on sportscasts throughout Canada. And they would read about it the next morning in sports sections from Halifax to Victoria.

"That's just great," Steve said when informed about his historic significance in the draft. "Those guys are great players. Bill Wennington just won a championship with the Bulls and that's the ultimate measure of any player. To be in the same category as him and Leo Rautins and Rick Fox and guys like that, it's just unbelievable."

Steve was well aware that he had become a beacon for the burgeoning number of basketball loving youngsters in Canada. He was a relatively average-sized player who had been developed through the Canadian basketball system. Kids shooting on driveway hoops from Charlottetown to Nanaimo could now point to him and say: "It's possible. It can be done."

"I'm tremendously proud to be Canadian," Steve said in an interview with Rod Black for CTV's nation-wide "Canada AM" the morning after the draft. "All you kids out there, you can accomplish anything you want. Just put your mind to it and be positive."

Steve would eventually survive the two-hour interview sessions on draft night and rejoin his family and friends in the lobby of the Sheraton Meadowlands. There, most of the drafted players mingled while preparing to motor off to their private celebrations. Steve's former Arbutus junior high teammate, Al Whitley, went to congratulate number one pick Allen Iverson with a handshake. Iverson threw his arms around Whitley and gave him a hug. Different worlds were meeting on this special night.

For Steve's group, the celebration was just beginning as they waited for cabs to take them to the trendy Spy Club in Greenwich Village. Once there, they would party the night away with New Jersey Nets forward Jayson Williams, who treated the celebrants to magnums of champagne and rounds of shooters. The draft-night party would eventually stretch into an early breakfast.

The other factor almost lost in the excitement of the draft was that Steve Nash had suddenly become an extremely wealthy young man. Under the NBA's rookie salary structure he would earn nearly $3.2 million US over the next three seasons. It was a guaranteed deal in which he would be paid even if he never played a single minute of an NBA game.

Steve's deal would pay him a base wage of $763,300 US in his rookie season, $877,800 in his second year and $992,300 in his third, as well as a 20 per cent bonus which would be secured by his agent Bill Duffy during contract negotiations. Allowing for about 40 per cent income tax, he would collect more than $45,000 a month. After four years of penny-pinching on an NCAA sports scholarship, Steve figured he would be able to get by on that.

But the money was pretty much an afterthought for Steve. A week after the draft, he was still being picked up by his friends in Victoria for afternoon basketball and weight sessions. He had yet to buy a car or anything else with his new-found wealth. He would be careful. He had heard many stories about athletes frittering away their fortunes.

Phoenix Suns president Jerry Colangelo and his first-round draft pick Steve Nash during July 24 press conference in Phoenix to announce the signing of a three-year $3.2 million deal.

In fact, Steve had decided that he would put away the vast majority of his earnings until he learned how to handle that volume of money. His father John, a marketing executive with Pacific Coast Savings credit union, would help him considerably, putting him on a budget and steering him toward the proper investments. So would his mother, Jean, who would also act as his business manager.

"I want to get a car," Steve said. "I mean, it'll be nice to have a car because I've never had one before. Other than that, I just want to find a place to live and be comfortable. I might have a few goodies but, other than a car and a house and a stereo, the list is pretty short. What can you get? There are only so many things to have in life."

Far more important than any money he was making was the fact that Steve had made it into the National Basketball Association. It was his biggest dream come true and the salary was a fringe benefit, albeit an extremely nice one.

"He's not going to be worried about how much money he's making because he just wants to play," said former Santa Clara teammate and point-guard mentor John Woolery. "If you just paid for all Steve's bills, he would play basketball for the rest of his life. He doesn't care about making a million dollars. He just wants to do this for the rest of his life. That's unique and that'll make him successful in the NBA."

A week after the draft, the excitement had died down around the Nash household. Steve Nash sprawled out on the couch in the family room, which was still decorated with the congratulatory balloon and flower arrangements that had arrived in the wake of draft day.

Steve had been mildly disappointed about not being flown directly into Phoenix on the day after the draft as seemed to be the custom in many NBA cities. But that disappointment had subsided after a one-day trip to Arizona for a media conference five days later. The highlight of the press conference had come when Steve was awarded a commemorative Suns' jersey with the number 96 on the back.

In the initial days following the draft, it had all seemed a little unreal to Steve. He had simply flown home to Victoria and, for the first time he could remember, he didn't really feel part of a team. But after his visit to Phoenix, armed with a rehab program scheduled by the Suns for his injured hamstring, he couldn't wait for the summer to be over.

Steve was keenly aware that he had passed into another phase in his life. Basketball would now officially be a job, not just a game. He could still love the sport as he had since he was a 13-year-old, but he had forever crossed that line of innocence separating pastime and business. And unlike most other university graduates going from their educational to career phases, Steve's transition would be a public one, available on television for all to see.

"Definitely it's a whole new thing," he admitted about entering the NBA. "You've got to prove yourself all over again. You've got to learn a whole bunch of things. You've got to gain respect. You're joining a new peer group, and everything's starting from scratch. It's really like going to the first day of high school again."

Steve would enter his first NBA training camp at Flagstaff, Arizona knowing that some Suns' fans didn't want him there and aware that he could still be part of a trade at any time. He would enter camp knowing that there were still doubts about his ability to ever replace Kevin Johnson as the Suns' starting point guard. In fact, there were still critics who doubted whether Steve had the quickness to be an NBA starter in any city. But he had survived the critics before. He was confident he would do so again. Confident enough, that when asked during a Phoenix press conference what kind of a player he'd be for the Suns, Steve joked: "Probably a little bit like Michael Jordan at first."

"I would refuse to put restrictions on him because he's always surpassed expectations," offered former Canadian national team coach Ken Shields. "Steve will bleed every ounce of potential

The three key ingredients in Steve Nash's success: a ball, a hoop and a dream.

out of his body and very few other players in the NBA will do that. Wherever he's gone, he's lived up to and gone beyond peoples' expectations. And he has the capacity to do that again."

The NBA would be a whole new challenge. But Steve was ready and eager for it. A week after achieving his wildest dreams upon a draft stage in New Jersey, he had set a whole new list of goals.

"I might be horrible the first three months, but I'm going to get better every single day. I'm going to raise my game to that level," Steve said.

"I know that if there is something I need to work on, like there always has been before, I'll work on it and I'll get it done. It's a big relief. I've made it, so to speak. I'm in the NBA now, so I'm relaxed," he continued. "But now I'm setting new goals. I want to win championships. I want to be an All-Star.

"I want to do it all."

And with that, Steve hopped off the couch and scavenged for his basketball shoes. His friends were picking him up in a couple of minutes. It was a gorgeous summer day and he was a 22-year-old millionaire, but Steve Nash was headed for the dusty old Oak Bay high school gym.

There were jumpers to hit. Maybe hundreds of them. Free throws, too. In Steve Nash's mind, the work wasn't really over at all.

It was only beginning.

Steve's Stats — The Nash Numbers

Stephen (Steve) John Nash
Guard — Phoenix Suns (drafted first round, 15th overall, June 1996)
College: Santa Clara University, Santa Clara, California
High School: St. Michaels University School, Victoria, British Columbia
Birthdate: February 7, 1974 (Johannesburg, South Africa)

Teams played for:
1988-1990 — Arbutus Junior Secondary School (Victoria, British Columbia),
1991-1992 — St. Michaels University School Blue Devils (Victoria, British Columbia)
1991 — Canadian Under-19 National Team
1992-93 — Canadian Student National Team
1993-95 — Canadian Senior National Team
1992-1996 — Santa Clara Broncos (Santa Clara, California)
1996-? — Phoenix Suns (Phoenix, Arizona)

Awards and Records — High School
First-team all-province, all-city and all-island honours
Most Valuable Player, Vancouver Island AAA Tournament
Most Valuable Player, British Columbia AAA Tournament
Times Colonist All-Star, B.C. under-17 team member
Per-game Averages: 21.3 points, 11.2 assists, 9.1 rebounds, 3.8 steals

Awards and Records — College
Two-time West Coast Conference Player of the Year (1994-95, 1995-96)
Two-time Wooden Award candidate
Honorable Mention All-America (Associated Press and United States Basketball Writers Association)
Santa Clara's all-time leader in career assists (510)
Santa Clara's third all-time leader career scorer (1,689)
Santa Clara's all-time leader (5th in NCAA) in free-throw shooting percentage (.861)
Three NCAA Tournament berths in four years
Career team record: 73-42
Per-game Averages: 14.9 points, 4.5 assists, 3.0 rebounds, 1.3 steals

Steve's Bronco Single-Game Highs

Points: 40, at Gonzaga, 1995

Field Goals: 11, at Gonzaga, 1995

Field Goal Attempts: 29, at Gonzaga, 1995

Three-point Field Goals: 8, at Gonzaga, 1995

Three-point Field Goal Attempts: 17, at Gonzaga, 1995

Free Throws: 21, vs. Saint Mary's, 1995

Free Throw Attempts: 21, vs. Saint Mary's, 1995

Rebounds: 8, twice, last vs. Maryland, 1996

Assists: 15, vs, Southern, 1995

Steals: 5, twice, last vs. Pepperdine, 1996

Minutes: 44, at Pacific, 1994

Santa Clara University (1992 - 1996)

YEAR	G-GS	MIN	FG-FGA	PCT	3FG-FGA	PCT	FT-FTA	PCT	REB-AVG	PF-D	A	TO	BK	ST	TP	AVG
92-93	31-5	743	78-184	.424	49-120	.408	47-57	.825	79-2.6	54-1	67	62	4	26	252	8.1
93-94	26-23	778	122-295	.414	67-167	.399	69-83	.831	65-2.5	57-1	95	74	1	34	380	14.6
94-95	27-27	902	164-369	.445	84-185	.454	153-174	.879	102-3.8	53-3	174	113	2	48	565	20.9
95-96	29-29	979	164-381	.431	63-183	.344	101-113	.894	103-3.6	43-0	174	103	0	39	492	17.0

Acknowledgements and Credits

The following people and organizations have been invaluable in helping to gather images for this book: Jean and John Nash, John W. McDonough, Christopher J. Relke, Eric Weinstein at NBA Photos, Marcia Lein Schiff at AP/Wide World Photos (AP), Ian Hyde-Lay, Jim Young at Santa Clara Sports Information (SCU-SI), Don Smith, and Sandy Grant at Canadian Sport Images (CSI).

Following is a list of photographs used, and the appropriate credits:

The author would like to thank the following people and organizations for their help with this project:

Polestar publisher Michelle Benjamin, for her strong belief in this book, her encouragement during the early stages and her tremendous support and guidance through its conclusion.

Steve Nash, for his patience, openness and accessibility during this project, a period when the demands on his time were many.

Jean and John Nash and the entire Nash family for their tremendous hospitality, co-operation and friendship during the year in which this book was put together; and for the extensive use of pictures and scrapbooks which were instrumental in piecing together *Long Shot*.

St. Michaels University School basketball coach Ian Hyde-Lay, for his enthusiastic co-operation and assistance telling Steve's story, through his high school days and beyond.

Polestar editor Kim Nash, for the thorough, thoughtful job she did on the manuscript.

Santa Clara head basketball coach Dick Davey, for his accessibility, co-operation and viewpoint during the writing and editing of this book.

Santa Clara Sports Information Director Jim Young and his staff, for their considerable help in chronicling Steve's career as a Bronco and for providing a wealth of statistics and game details.

Santa Clara photographer Don Smith, for providing an extensive selection of photos of Steve in action as a Bronco.

Ken Shields, for his help telling Steve's story with the Canadian national team program.

Victoria *Times Colonist* sports editor Dave Senick, for his understanding and flexibility and for often going out of his way to enable the author to make research trips during the 1995-96 basketball season.

Norm LeBus, Victoria journalist and basketball fan, for his sharp eye and volunteer editing work.

The Phoenix Suns, for their co-operation in providing information and photographs for this book.

Jeff Rud is a sports columnist with the Victoria *Times Colonist*, and has also covered basketball for *USA Today* and CBC Television's *The Score*. *Long Shot* is his first book. He lives in Victoria, British Columbia.